WHY FAITH?

A Journey of Discovery

MATT EMERSON

Paulist Press
New York / Mahwah, NJ

Cover image by Vera In August Fine Photography
Cover design by Phyllis Campos
Book design by Lynn Else

Library of Congress Cataloging-in-Publication Data

Emerson, Matt.
    Why faith? : a journey of discovery / Matt Emerson.
      pages cm
    Includes bibliographical references.
    ISBN 978-0-8091-4941-4 (pbk. : alk. paper) — ISBN 978-1-58768-532-3 (ebook)
    1. Catholic Church—Doctrines. 2. Theology, Doctrinal—Popular works. 3. Faith.
I. Title.
    BX1754.E47 2016
    230'.2—dc23

                                              2015022790

ISBN 978-0-8091-4941-4 (paperback)
ISBN 978-1-58768-532-3 (e-book)

Published by Paulist Press
997 Macarthur Boulevard
Mahwah, New Jersey 07430

www.paulistpress.com

Printed and bound in the
United States of America

To
Natalie, Mom, Dad, and Pat
for your love, faith, and support

Contents

Acknowledgments

Writing this book began not long after my engagement to my wife, Natalie, to whom I owe the greatest gratitude for her commitment and love. She helped me with difficult chapters, read early drafts, and strengthened my belief in this project when the finish line seemed impossibly far off. I am honored to be her husband.

I am forever thankful to my parents, Richard and Mary Emerson, and my brother, Patrick, for providing a loving foundation for my own search for God and for keeping my writing grounded in real human concerns. They challenge me in all the right ways and inspire me to seek excellence.

I thank David Gregory for his outstanding feedback on so many chapters, as well as Fr. Brian Daley, SJ, and Dr. Carey Walsh, who helped me navigate some of the finer points of Catholic theology. I am grateful to Fr. Matt Malone, SJ, Karen Sue Smith, Kerry Weber, Luke Hansen, and the team at *America* for giving me space to write about many of the subjects that appear in this book. I am also grateful to Jimmy Tricco, Chris Alling, Dave and Sheila Thornton, and Laura, Katie, and Keira Thornton for their cheerful encouragement throughout this project.

Thank you especially to Paulist Press and to my editor, Paul McMahon, who patiently guided me through the inevitable roadblocks and impasses, keeping me on track but giving me the freedom to wrestle with the big ideas. For his keen eye and patient support, I am most grateful.

Introduction:
FROM INNER STRUGGLE
TO SAVING GRACE

A former student of mine once wrote me after attending a four-day retreat. Reflecting on the few days she had dwelled in solitude, she expressed appreciation for the prayerful getaway, but added, "My relationship with God is the struggling element of my life."

"Struggling element": her words moved but didn't surprise me. As a theology teacher at a Jesuit high school, I hear such sentiments often. But it's not only high school students who work through these questions and struggle with spirituality. Men and women of all ages and backgrounds frequently express a sorrowful frustration in their spiritual searches. The idea of God, as well as the beliefs, rituals, and practices that make up the Christian faith, often confuse, intimidate, and overwhelm. Occasionally, people might enjoy spiritual peace or relish a mystical presence, but it's often fleeting, and not sufficient to create any lasting commitment or shift in plans.

This difficulty arises for various reasons, and usually out of a mix of experiences, prejudices, intuitions, and assumptions. Many conclude that whoever or whatever God might be, the thought of believing in a God is so complex, so burdened with mystery and uncertainty, that it is too daunting to try. For many in today's culture, God holds a reputation similar to that of Bigfoot or the Loch Ness monster. Some claim he is real, but there remains so much superstition and disagreement that God—so the argument goes—is not worth taking seriously. The images are too shadowy, too grainy; perhaps a lucky few glimpse him, but they cannot verify their claims.

The number of religions and worldviews enhances these difficulties. My students often wonder, "How can one religion be right if so many claim to be true?" The diversity of beliefs and rituals makes it seem unnecessary, even unethical, to choose one religious path over another. Facing this variety, many people assume the world's religions are equally valid: the dharma in Hinduism as legitimate as the Trinity of Christianity; and the five pillars of Islam no less important than the four noble truths of Buddhism.

Sometimes, however, it's the opposite. Sometimes people believe the world's religions not to be equally true and inspiring, but rather, to be untrue and absurd. Because of the behavior of predatory priests, many people associate Catholic Christianity with sexual abuse. Because of the 9/11 terrorist attacks and other massacres around the globe, countless people connect Islam to violence. The wars in the Middle East, incited in part by religious disagreements, tend to confirm the skepticism. Television audiences see the smoke rising from a rocket attack and bodies lying in the streets and equate faith with fanaticism. Rather than being viewed as a center of love and community, as the source of water for the parched lips of the poor, faith is linked with parents grieving over coffins. People question, "How can God allow suffering on such a scale?"

There is also the "strangeness" of religion. Every genuine religious experience contains an element of otherness; something that cuts through the center of what our normal, this-world mind deems true or acceptable. There is always some aspect that unsettles and perhaps leaves us thinking, "How can this be?" Consider the basic outline of Catholic Christianity:

God the Almighty, creator of heaven and earth, comes to earth through a young Jewish mother named Mary, under what, at the time, are highly questionable, even scandalous, circumstances.

This God-in-the-flesh, whom an angel names Jesus (meaning "God saves"), has a relatively conventional human life until around the age of thirty, at which time he begins a public ministry filled with awe-inspiring healings, exorcisms, and other miracles. Furthermore, he spreads a message of heroic love and virtue, and proclaims that the kingdom of God is at hand.

During his ministry, his words and actions both intrigue and appall his contemporaries. Eventually, Jesus' behavior so angers the Jewish religious authorities, who believe him to be committing blasphemy, that they have him arrested and put on trial before the Jewish Supreme Court. After this court convicts Jesus, it hands him over to the Roman authorities, who, based on a false political charge, sentence him to be crucified.

However, as terrible as this death is, it isn't the end. Jesus rises from the dead, demonstrating the triumph of good over evil and the possibility of everlasting life. After this magnificent, one-of-a-kind event, which Christians celebrate each year at Easter, he appears to his followers and asks them to spread his message to the world.

As part of the journey to holiness and faith, and in response to Jesus' life and teachings, his followers must gather to hear stories (what Christians call the *Gospels*) about Jesus, as well as to eat his body and drink his blood at the Eucharist—not symbolically his body and blood, but truly and actually his body and blood. But the flesh and the blood that we consume don't look like flesh and blood; rather, they appear as bread and wine. Mystically, in ways we cannot fathom, the bread and wine, through the action of the priest, are changed into the body and blood of Christ.

In addition to this regular gathering, which Catholics call *Mass* or *Eucharist*, Jesus' (God's) presence persists with the community of believers through the action of the Holy Spirit, who forms one "person" of what Christians proclaim as the Holy Trinity. The *Trinity* is the term that refers to one God in the form of three persons: Father, Son, and Holy Spirit.

Every person is invited to embody the teachings of Jesus and to proclaim the message of the gospel, taught by the apostles and the early Church.

This abbreviated account of the events of Jesus' life and subsequent history is not always easy to accept. Some of it might even disturb (eat his flesh and drink his blood?). These are not stories or teachings that immediately ring true, that integrate seamlessly with our typical human experience, either now or twenty centuries ago. Combine these hard-to-believe claims about God in the flesh with Christianity's strong moral demands, and it's no mystery why people turn away or decide not to believe. Intellectually and emotionally, the whole project seems to ask too much.

This book is my response to the struggle, my effort to make faith, particularly Catholic Christianity, accessible for the modern seeker. It is my conviction that the story I've outlined above, as incredible as it sounds, is true, and that when it comes to faith, far too many people are unnecessarily befuddled and demoralized, and for far too long. Therefore, to bring clarity and foster hope, this book attempts to convey the belief that Christianity is worth giving our whole lives to. To this purpose, the following points should be noted.

First, this book is not intended as a defense of Catholicism or Christianity, a work of "apologetics," as such titles are often known. I am not trying to argue the reader into submission or remove all doubts about the subject at hand. Rather, I share the fruits of my own experiences and contemplations.

Second, it is not a general introduction to the Christian faith. The subject of Catholic Christianity spans limitless ideas, topics, and people, and implicates theology, history, philosophy, archaeology, language, and additional scholarly fields. There are countless books, some very good, that attempt such a grand overview. Rather than undertake such a daunting task, this book focuses on a few key areas to show why and how we can entrust ourselves to Christ.

Third, a good portion of this book focuses not only on the object of our search—specific themes of Catholic Christianity— but also on the subjects who embark upon that search: the men and women who must work out the questions of faith in their lives. Too often, we rush to answer questions without understanding the audience who asks them. It's like a basketball coach trying to install an offense without inquiring, "Have my players ever played basketball? Do they know what the game is all about? Have they ever been on a team before?" If the coach doesn't address these preliminary matters, if he doesn't address the context and the culture that form his players, he will not succeed. He will assume too much or too little. He will not meet his players where they have the greatest need.

Finally, this book is intended for the modern seeker. By "modern" I mean that person shaped by the culture of the twenty-first century: the world of Google and YouTube, of Instagram and Snapchat, of LeBron James and reality TV—someone who has come to adulthood post–9/11, during the age of social media and the dominance of the smartphone. It is for those persons who are seeking the truth about themselves, about God, and about humanity, searching for meaning beyond the surface of their immediate experience. It is for those who detect "a certain perception of that hidden power which hovers over the course of things and over the events of human history," but for whom faith feels too much like the way calculus felt to me—near impossible. Consequently, what follows will resonate with people who wish to deepen their faith but who find spirituality a struggle.

Inspirations

While based on my own reading and ideas, this book has emerged primarily from my quest to understand God and my efforts to make sense of Catholic Christianity—and religion in general. This quest has included nineteen years of Catholic education, stretching from my Catholic elementary school in Phoenix through law school at the University of Notre Dame. While not a professional philosopher or theologian, I am an "informed believer" who continues to participate in the questions this book addresses.

More recently, the ideas and questions in this book have found inspiration from the conversations I have had with students whom I've had the honor of teaching over the past six years. Smart and inquisitive, these young men and women have rarely been prepared to accept the claims of Christianity, let alone any religion. The chapters that follow are the fruits of thousands of discussions from theology classes, in which students have pursued the most intricate of inquiries, rejecting anything that has the glimmer of platitude or cliché. Put simply, this book has emerged from an environment where the value of religion has not been presumed, where the cherished doctrines of Christianity have had to be defended almost every day.

Consequently, some chapters will address matters that are clearly theological, while others will address more philosophical and sociological topics. Such questions include the following: What does it mean to search for God in the context of the twenty-first century? What is faith? What does it mean to entrust ourselves to a reality we cannot fully understand?

While primarily for the modern seeker, this book is also for skeptics who aren't convinced of their skepticism and for the disciple looking to strengthen his or her "yes" to God. It's for teachers and students, for moms and dads, for the person who settles into his or her commute with big questions on the mind. All of us, no matter our age or beliefs, know the cry of the grieving father in the Gospel of Mark: "I believe; help my unbelief!" (9:24).

In what follows, it is my hope to do exactly that: to show how our lives of faith can be enriching and life-giving, and to provide a road map for how faith can move from struggle to saving grace.

Really?

CHAPTER ONE

A Journey of Discovery

On St. Patrick's Day 2013, Gregory, a former student of mine, fell backward from a skateboard as he whisked down a street at high speed. He landed on his head, not wearing a helmet. The paramedics arrived within minutes and immediately placed Greg on life support.

In the days after his fall, friends and family, teachers and doctors, and dozens of others within Greg's circle gathered at the hospital. We knelt over his bed and whispered encouragements to recovery. On the sloping damp grass outside the window of his room, with sun shining through palm trees, we prayed rosaries and gripped hands. Strangers consoled each other like new-found family.

During that week and for months following, everyone connected to Greg's life confronted some of the most difficult questions that face human beings. Realities and fears we often suppress—death, the fragility of life, the persistence

1

of suffering—suddenly became urgent. It was a time, as my friend would say, of "the 3 a.m. phone call."

What is the 3 a.m. phone call? The 3 a.m. phone call refers to those moments that jar us from our literal and even figurative sleep. They are moments that awake us from the autopilot of routine, from the unmemorable normality that fills most of our days. After the 3 a.m. phone call, we take leave of trivialities and small concerns, and return to those matters that alone can break our hearts or make us whole.

This call often involves something sad, but it could also arise from something quite wonderful. It can emerge from the cries of a delivery room or the words of a proposal. It can originate in the news of a promotion or in the news of a health scare that turns out to be only a scare.

Just recently, a good friend of mine expressed to me how her life had completely changed because of the birth of her first child. "You need to have a kid ASAP," she wrote. "It will change your life."

Regardless of the cause, the 3 a.m. phone call compels us to reflect upon who we are, what we value, and how we frame the purpose of our lives. We're no longer worried about what we're wearing, what we drive, or how big our houses are. We are suddenly united with the rest of the human family in essential concerns. The 3 a.m. phone call turns us into philosophers. We ask questions that great thinkers have posed for centuries: Who am I? Why are we here? What is happiness? Why do we exist? What does it mean to be a parent? What example do I want to leave my child?

For example, after my friend gave birth to her daughter, she began to rethink her career. For years, she had told herself she wanted to be a lawyer, but eventually she acknowledged that her heart wasn't in it. When she became a mother, everything was different. She began to reevaluate the life and decision-making she wanted to model for her child. These considerations eventually caused her to leave the practice of law and start a career that better reflected what she truly desired.

The questions and contemplations of the 3 a.m. phone call are never more urgent than in the wake of tragedy, particularly after the death of a friend or loved one. As my friends and colleagues lingered outside the hospital for news about Greg's condition, many wondered whether we would see him again, and if so, where. Does God exist? Are our prayers working? Is there life after death?

It is in these uncertain moments—the moments of the 3 a.m. phone call—that we begin to wonder about a meaning beyond what we ourselves construct. We begin to wonder about truths that are ultimate and final, that supersede our day-to-day concerns. It is here that we arrive at the border of religious belief and the life of faith. It is religious belief that attempts to answer our big questions in ways that satisfy, not for fleeting moments, but for our entire lives. It is religious belief that attempts to direct our questions and longings into a set of principles, beliefs, and morals that we know as a "worldview," which will, like a strong relationship, keep us steady through the storms and waves of life—through the highs and lows of 3 a.m. phone calls and the life that happens in between.

Authentic religious belief begins not with people who want to flee reality, but with people who want to move more fully into it. Too often, people assume religion involves closed systems of thought that restrict free and rigorous inquiry. While those systems exist, that description fails to reflect the broader religious landscape, especially that of Catholic Christianity. In my experience, religious people aren't primarily those who claim to have answers; rather, they are people who persistently ask questions. They are people who possess a curiosity that enables them to

entertain mystery and to remain open to new insights and dis-
coveries.

Religious people see dogma and doctrine and the more challenging practices of religion as providing a means of talking
about, approaching, and respecting the mystery, which nevertheless remains wholly transcendent.

L of Life

A Journey of Discovery

Faith, religion, and God are not topics for those who want to
flee reality or shut down rational thinking. They arise naturally in
response to the events of our lives. Whether we acknowledge
them or not, the questions of the 3 a.m. phone call always linger
near our minds. As Greg's friends and family discovered so terri-
bly, at any moment, they can be awakened.

So, what are we to make of these big questions? What attitude do they invite from us? Are they riddles? Are they pieces to
a puzzle? Can we answer whatever we want, without any thought
to resources outside ourselves?

In reflecting on these questions, I offer the following guidance from St. John Paul II, who spent most of his life wrestling
with the great questions of human existence, who lived through
his own 3 a.m. moments, including the Nazi invasion of his native
Poland in 1939 and an attempt on his life in 1984. Writing in a
1998 letter to members of the Catholic Church, John Paul stated:

> A glance at ancient history shows clearly how in differ-
> ent parts of the world, with their different cultures,
> there arise at the same time the fundamental questions
> which pervade human life: Who am I? Where have I
> come from and where am I going? Why is there evil?
> What is there after this life?...These are the questions
> which we find in the sacred writings of Israel, as also in

No How?

4

external

the Veda and the Avesta; we find them in the writings of Confucius and Lao-Tze, and in the preaching of Tirthankara and Buddha; they appear in the poetry of Homer and in the tragedies of Euripides and Sophocles, as they do in the philosophical writings of Plato and Aristotle.[1]

For St. John Paul II, seeking answers to these questions is not something reserved for scholars hunched over books or for those people jamming flyers under your windshield wipers. It is not reserved for philosophy or theology majors. Rather, John Paul said that the search to answer these questions amounts to a "journey of discovery." It is a journey, he wrote, that "has led humanity down the centuries to meet and engage truth more and more deeply...to discover ever new frontiers of knowledge."[2]

This journey of discovery is a journey not only for Buddha and Socrates, or for popes and professors. It's a journey for you, for me, for my students who sat outside Greg's hospital room, and for every other man and woman who has ever lived. Each of us receives the 3 a.m. phone call. *Maybe!*

The Crucial Choice

Given this journey, we face a choice. <u>What shall we do?</u> If the search for truth and meaning is a journey of discovery, will we say yes or will we turn away, assuming it's of no value, assuming that we cannot discover the ultimate truth about the nature of God, the nature of ourselves, and the nature of the world we live in? In other words, we can take the <u>questions</u> seriously and make their investigation part of our lives, or we can ignore them. The choice is ours. *Why?*

If we choose to embark on this journey, we must do so with total dedication. Many people express interest in knowing more about the Christian faith, or about God, but remain totally convinced of their own preconceived notions. They are unwilling to read, unwilling to investigate, unwilling to ask tough questions and hear answers that might require them to change their minds. Such people abandon their interest in faith because it doesn't immediately make sense or because it seems too hard. Some people, burdened by personal misfortune, simply have no patience for the possibility of God.

Catholic Christianity, like any religion, cannot be mastered with occasional conversations, a few Google searches, or a review of a Wikipedia page. We cannot treat the life of faith, the questions that have spanned centuries, the same way we often treat our plans for physical health. How often do we talk about improving our bodies or eating habits without committing to a plan? How often do we engage in a few weeks of jogging and weightlifting, only to default to a pattern of inactivity?

To gain clarity about faith and about God—to enhance our spiritual health—we face a similar choice. Faith has to be something we care about, not a project that we're going to dismiss after a few weeks, like a half-completed painting. It has to be something that deeply affects us, a journey we approach with an open mind and heart, ready to follow truth wherever it leads.

Yes we can!

No it doesn't.

CHAPTER TWO

The Language of Self-Surrender

A few weeks before I graduated from law school, I developed a pain behind my right eye. It wouldn't go away, and so after my last exams, I went to the doctor. I saw two optometrists who peered into my eyeballs with machines that looked like NASA had built them. In the deep space of my head, these devices found nothing alarming. One of the doctors said my discomfort might be caused by dry eye. For the next few weeks, I used eye drops multiple times a day, but nothing changed.

I visited another doctor, and he, too, found nothing obviously wrong. Just to be sure, however, he ordered a magnetic resonance imaging (MRI) of my brain to rule out a tumor. The MRI came back normal, but the pain persisted.

At that time, the bar exam was only about six weeks away and required constant studying, so I needed answers. The pain was interrupting my sleeping and my reading. A few weeks into the search, I saw a neurologist noted for his brilliance. He began his examination unlike most typical doctors. He asked me about my history with headaches as well as that of my family. He asked me about what I ate and drank—how much caffeine, alcohol, chocolate—and he wanted to know what my life had been like during the time the pain set in. Was I under any stress?

I thought it was a bit odd; I had eye pain. Who cared what I was eating?

He took notes as I spoke, said little, and then, after a few seconds of silence, he looked up and told me the news: "It's a migraine."

What? A migraine?

Migraine pain, he said, can cause all kinds of aches that are otherwise mysterious. He said I had inherited the migraine gene, which stress, anxiety, and poor diet could activate.

And then I knew: When my pain started, I was studying for my final set of law school exams and anticipating the stress of the bar exam. I was drinking gallons of coffee and my only exercise was a short walk to and from the library. There were other issues, too, that made my mind feel like an overstuffed suitcase. Something had to give.

My doctor, the neurologist, prescribed medication, and overnight the pain went away.

My experience with the migraine was instructive for many reasons, especially for the way it taught me about the importance of context. Until I saw the neurologist, no one had asked me about the decisions and behaviors that accompanied the onset of pain. While previous doctors were well intentioned, they didn't ask the right questions. They were working within a paradigm and with assumptions that were unable to detect what was truly at stake.

8

This tale of my migraine is a helpful analogy for the subject of the spiritual life. Just as context and circumstances shape medical questions, so too do they impact our spiritual questions. When Greg's friends and peers gathered at the hospital, they did so as young men and women conditioned by the circumstances of their ages and places. Some came from religious families; others did not. Some played water polo, while others participated in mock trial. They listened to musical artists like Of Monsters and Men, One Direction, The Lumineers, and Beyoncé. They carried smartphones with near-constant access to Twitter, Facebook, and the Internet.

Like our medical struggles, therefore, spiritual struggles have to be understood within a specific culture of living and decision-making. Otherwise, we labor with misconceptions or bounce from authority to authority without gaining any answers.

As we commence this journey of discovery, we must ask the following: What is the context in which this faith journey occurs? What are the circumstances within which our spiritual questions arise? Do we even have spiritual questions at all? In other words, for the modern seeker, what are the forces and factors that shape what and how we think?

Belief and Culture

In the introduction, I mentioned my student's comment that God was the "struggling element" of her life. While her comment was true, it was also incomplete. It isn't just belief in God that is a struggling element. All beliefs are difficult. All beliefs force us to wrestle with mystery, complexity, and variety. Any intellectual commitment beyond trivial matters confronts opposing forces and clashing voices. In any journey we take, there are competing paths.

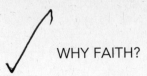

WHY FAITH?

In his book *The Paradox of Choice: Why More is Less*, Barry Schwartz wrote about the time he went to a Gap store to buy jeans:

> A nice young salesperson walked up to me and asked if she could help.
>
> "I want a pair of jeans—32-28," I said.
>
> "Do you want them slim fit, easy fit, relaxed fit, baggy, or extra baggy?" she replied. "Do you want them stonewashed, acid-washed, or distressed? Do you want them button-fly or zipper-fly? Do you want them faded or regular?"
>
> I was stunned. A moment or two later I sputtered out something like, "I just want regular jeans. You know, the kind that used to be the only kind." It turned out she didn't know, but after consulting one of her older colleagues, she was able to figure out what "regular" jeans used to be, and she pointed me in the right direction.
>
> The trouble was that with all these options available to me now, I was no longer sure that "regular" jeans were what I wanted. Perhaps the easy fit or the relaxed fit would be more comfortable. Having already demonstrated how out of touch I was with modern fashion, I persisted. I went back to her and asked what difference there was between regular jeans, relaxed fit, and easy fit. She referred me to a diagram that showed how the different cuts varied. It didn't help narrow the choice, so I decided to try them all.[1]

Schwartz's experience of buying jeans is an apt parable for what it's like to be human. To be human is to be embedded in rival worldviews that complicate what we know or wish to be true. To be human is to confront personalities and ideologies that constantly test our convictions, leaving us tempted to try on all different kinds of viewpoints, religions, and systems of thought.

Even our own selves, our own inner sanctuaries of loves and

10

interests, can present themselves as a language we cannot translate. There are days we look in the mirror and wonder, "Who are you?" or perhaps, "*What* are you?" In our search and effort to remain faithful to something unchanging, we empathize with the words of Stanley Kunitz, who wrote,

> I have walked through many lives,
> some of them my own,
> and I am not who I was,
> though some principle of being
> abides, from which I struggle
> not to stray.[2]

We search for this "principle of being," but it's hard to find. Throughout our lives, we evolve, change, and grow.

Our own families are increasingly diverse, linked by few shared values. Parents and children often hold different opinions on fundamental matters or hold no views at all. God, friendship, commitment, love, and education—on these issues and more, people's thoughts often lack "togetherness" or intentionality. As a consequence, a great many people drift in and out of assumptions without developing lasting convictions.

To be alive in the twenty-first century is to be beckoned to buy, to think of ourselves primarily as spenders. The world is a Gap store, and we are constantly buying jeans. In the ancient world, we were *spiritual* beings; now we are *consumers*. Advertisements compete for attention, and companies crave loyalty. Businesses hawk reward cards and membership programs. Netflix, Hulu, and cable television conglomerates constantly ask for subscriptions. Features like Amazon's "one-click purchasing" enable us to purchase almost anything with, literally, one click. Modern consumerism makes spending money as effortless as changing channels.

Interesting

What receives our attention? For many, Facebook or Twitter is the primary source of news and information. Increasingly, people expect that whatever is worth knowing about will find them, not the other way around. If something doesn't materialize after opening a browser, if it doesn't arise in a news feed or through a hyperlink, people might never hear about it. More and more, search results determine value. What about wisdom that algorithms cannot capture? The idea that knowledge is hard work, that insight into life and humanity takes time, and that it might require many years and the enduring of disappointments fades away behind an endless stream of tweets, posts, and user-uploaded videos.

We manipulate. Photo-editing programs enable us to cut, crop, and filter. We become thinner in some places, bigger in others, and tweak for smooth skin, smaller thighs, and whiter teeth. A few clicks and swipes create exactly what we want, in the image and likeness of ourselves.

Noise and activity surround us without ceasing. What one of my high school teachers once asked me remains compelling today: "When are you in total silence? When do you go without noise?"

From the moment we arise to the moment we fall asleep, we are rarely alone, and rarely able to enjoy a restoring calm. Sometimes, of course, there is good reason. Moms and dads, after all, don't have the luxury of letting their five-year-olds cook their own dinners. Students can't cut class. But even acknowledging those responsibilities, we often don't seize opportunities to be silent.

The ways we structure our streams of information and edit for conformity to our desires lead to virtual gated communities. The more we enclose ourselves in these communities, the more we think the whole world looks, acts, and thinks like the people surrounding us—those who "like" and share and attach smiley faces to what we say or photograph. We forget about other people, other opinions, and other ways of living. Do we even know they exist?

Complete negativity, however, is not called for. It is tempting for every generation to lament the decline of morals and education, but in the spirit of honest critique, we cannot ignore the good things this new era brings.

These are inspiring times for the same reasons they are troublesome. If this is an age of diminished attention spans, it's also an age of empowerment. From Boston to Beijing, men and women of all backgrounds can retrieve information at a pace previously unimagined. Many students come to freshman year in high school with skills that once required thousands of dollars and a college degree. They can build computers, design video games, and learn languages, and they can do so without paying a dime.[3] They are browsing their way into innovative connections between math and computers, between photography and digital art, between history and film. Online education organizations like the Khan Academy and Skillshare teach people about graphic design, history, math, finance, and more. Massive Open Online Courses (MOOCs) have connected schools like Stanford and Harvard to those who live thousands of miles away from a campus.

Technological advances have rapidly increased the speed and accuracy with which we access information. It is now possible to get an answer to most questions in seconds—directions to the grocery store, the temperature in Barcelona, Latin conjugations, Act 5 of *Hamlet*, articles, videos, pictures, and more. E-readers, like the Kindle from Amazon and the iPad from Apple, make access to books quicker and cheaper than ever before. With the arrival of Siri, it's even more astonishing—a computerized voice can be instructed to read and send messages, make phone calls, tell the score of the Notre Dame game, and provide the weather forecast.

Today, entrepreneurs can build their own websites overnight and reach customers within days. Facebook, YouTube, and Twitter give start-ups endless free marketing and have removed many of the barriers that once guarded the marketplace.

Scientific and medical breakthroughs continue to astound and to illuminate mysteries that had baffled humans for centuries. Breakthroughs in physics and chemistry can tell us what happened about fourteen billion years ago, within fractions of seconds of the cosmic explosion we know as the "Big Bang." Doctors and scientists report growing successes in blocking the transmission of HIV and in curing other diseases. In fact, there have been advances in brain implants, or what doctors call neuroprosthetics—"devices that restore or supplement the mind's capacities with electronics inserted directly into the nervous system."[4] The miraculous, it seems, is close at hand.

Our Background Theories

When it comes to God, the circumstances outlined above, though not exhaustive, provide the setting—the intellectual and conceptual "base camp"—in which our faith journey begins. We have no access to faith apart from the time and place in which we exist, apart from the encounters and experiences that form the plotlines of our lives. Our cultures, our families, and our own inner worlds create a unique lens through which we encounter and interpret reality.

Everything that comprises our context creates certain attitudes and dispositions. It fosters a certain way of living and perceiving. And these attitudes and dispositions—this way of living and perceiving—form what a former professor of mine once

(Intellectual

called "background theories," the unstated assumptions and cluster of opinions that shape our judgments about the world. They are often unacknowledged, acting as the implicit grounds for our decisions and choices. Background theories help us determine what we believe, what we value, and how we react to ideas, people, and daily life. They can impact, for good or ill, our journeys of discovery and our searches for faith.

For example, consider the culture created by the Internet and smartphones. The more we use these technologies, the more our minds are conditioned to their immediate access to information, so that we can start to assume that all knowledge should come with the ease of a Google search: we input a question and, within seconds, we receive an answer or at least a "result."

When this becomes the primary way of learning, it can start to form a background theory. That background theory might be described by the following principles: *Knowledge should come to me with immediacy. If the answers I'm looking for don't show up on the first page of search results, they are either not worth seeking or they don't exist.*

In time, we can become passive and inactive. Instead of approaching knowledge with care and diligence, we start to view it as something that requires little sacrifice or exertion. We start to rely on the intellectual equivalent of fast food.

This background theory, however, can cause problems when we start to theorize about God and about the possibilities for a life of faith. Like the study of history or law or any other field of inquiry, studying Christianity requires reading, thinking, and discerning. The claims of Christianity intersect with language, history, archaeology, philosophy, and more, and their study is rewarding but demanding.

Additionally, the Christian faith is intended to be embodied. It is not enough to hear or read about the call of God; the point is to respond to it. Starting with the call of Abraham in Genesis, the first book of the Bible, and continuing with the call of Jesus' apostles much later in the New Testament, the journey into a relationship with God is never easy, immediate, or obvious. It's a relationship, according to the scriptures, that usually brings a period of testing, wandering, and sometimes even frustration.

The well-known encounter between Jesus and the "rich young man," reported in three of the four Gospels, illustrates the point. In this story from the New Testament, a wealthy man asks Jesus how to gain everlasting life. Jesus tells him to follow the Ten Commandments but adds, "If you wish to be perfect, go, sell your possessions, and give the money to the poor, and you will have treasure in heaven; then come, follow me" (Matt 19:21).

Jesus leaves it at that. He doesn't offer additional explanation, but rather keeps it open-ended: *Follow me.* Follow him where? For how long? And why? You can imagine the questions that haunt the rich man. *Where am I going? Will I make any money? What about my family? Can I trust you? What about my other plans?*

The story ends without answers to those questions. According to the scriptures, what is important is not that we know exactly how life will unfold, but rather that we are willing to say yes to Jesus' call. We must be willing to surrender to a mystery and embark upon a path that might, at first, leave us feeling fearful and unprepared, maybe even resentful. In fact, according to the Gospel story: "When the young man heard this word, he went away grieving, for he had many possessions" (Matt 19:22).

To be in relationship with God, therefore, doesn't mean that one has it all figured out; it doesn't mean that answers to life's big questions will be delivered with precision. It means the same thing that every other healthy and loving relationship means: clarity unfolds gradually and depends upon trust, patience, courage, and humility. It means that we have to set aside the language of self-empowerment for the language of self-surrender.

With that in mind, consider again the background theories we develop in a culture of Siri, Google, and YouTube. "Mystery," "sacrifice," and "uncertainty" generally have no place in the vocabularies of these companies. This doesn't mean those companies lack value. For certain purposes, they are outstanding. However, their contributions come with a cost: our constant use of them eats away at the attentive, courageous engagement that faith requires.

Take the example of prayer. According to the traditional Jewish and Christian understanding, God is the creator of all and is, therefore, necessarily incomprehensible. God far outstrips the capacity of the human being to understand his ways. No satellite or microprocessor can capture God's will. There is no spiritual version of one-click purchasing that will deliver God on demand.

However, in a context where immediacy is the norm, do we have the patience to pray, to wait, and to listen? In prayer, it's not necessarily the case that God will respond right away or in the manner we demand. In an age of instant answers and incessant clicking of links, we may have to exhibit a degree of patience; a patience uncharacteristic of a hyper-consuming, immediately gratifying culture. If God exists and loves me, God may have something in mind that surpasses what I could imagine.

Our Prior Judgments

Sometimes it's not clear what causes our background theories or assumptions. It might not be something as elaborate as "the culture," but simply our own reactions to the world, the results of our own family dynamics, or our unique constellations of experiences and intuitions.

During one of my senior theology classes a few years ago, my class began discussing Eben Alexander's *Proof of Heaven: A*

Neurosurgeon's Near-Death Experience and Journey into the Afterlife. In this work, Alexander offers a detailed account of his near-death experience, explaining how he encountered his long-deceased sister in another dimension.

After discussing some of the compelling facts of the book, I asked the class whether they believed Dr. Alexander's account and whether the afterlife exists.

Arguing passionately that Dr. Alexander had neither seen any glimpse of heaven nor gained any proof of an afterlife, one of my students was convinced that such an experience was impossible. When I questioned this student about his assumptions, he dug in further. When I challenged him with evidence from the book and asked him once more for the basis of his belief, he said loudly and with a bit of irritation, "I just don't want it to be true."

In other words, the student didn't want to consider evidence that might undermine his prior judgments. He had approached the subject of heaven with a background theory that ruled out the possibility of an afterlife. He had come to the discussion with a narrative through which he wanted to filter information. When I pointed out that his wish, rather than openness to truth, was driving his response to Dr. Alexander, my student acknowledged he might have to reconsider his view.

When it comes to faith, we often draw many conclusions based on what we wish to be true rather than what is true. In fairness, those who possess religious faith can just as easily do the same. For example, some Christians remain resolutely committed to an interpretation of the early chapters of the Bible (the Creation stories) that is inconsistent with the overwhelming consensus of modern science.

When we live on unexamined background theories or on preconceived notions, we base our lives on ideas that may be false or only partially true. This doesn't mean that we should eliminate background theories entirely. It's impossible to live without some kind of philosophical stance toward the world, some basic set of values and beliefs we don't have to constantly revisit or re-verify. However, when we rest comfortably on what we *want* to be the case, rather than searching for what *is* the case, we risk living within illusions. For centuries, people thought the sun revolved around the earth and that the universe was only a few thousand years old. These were background theories that few people challenged. And yet once people contested those theories and offered evidence to support new ideas, accepted assumptions changed. In the face of new evidence, new convictions had to form.

Are you open to the same in your spiritual life? Do you carry a religious belief that remains unexamined or outdated? Do you care to investigate the truth of the matter?

The Ultimate Goal

Reviewing the context in which our faith journey begins also invites us to clarify our intentions concerning God and the spiritual life. What are we seeking? What do we wish to know?

In July 2008, the night after the first day of the Arizona bar exam, a friend, who was also taking the exam, joined me for dinner. He had recently married and had his first child. I asked him if he and his wife attended Mass any more. After a few seconds, he said, "No." He then added, "You know, we could be Jewish, and I wouldn't care." When I asked why, his answer jumped from one objection to another. He thought no one religion was truer than another, and so we couldn't be too certain about the divinity of Jesus. In trying to address some of his concerns, he turned from fundamental objections about the nature of religion to more specific critiques of the Catholic Church, which, he claimed, mistreats women, holds too strong to tradition, and ignores the teachings of the Second Vatican Council.

His response befuddled me. What was the reason for his difficulties? Was it that all religions were equally true or was it something related to Catholicism? If the Catholic Church were to ordain women, allow priests to marry, and modernize more aggressively, would that have changed anything?

Although we didn't talk further about his relationship with Catholicism, his words stayed with me for months. The conversation typified many of the encounters I've had about faith. Often, someone who knows I teach theology and write on theological subjects will ask me about Jesus or some other aspect of the Christian faith. I will try to provide the best answer I can, but as soon as I answer one question, another question is raised. But it's not so much a question as a critique. They are questions suited for cross-examination: How can you really prove that Jesus rose from the dead? Why doesn't the Catholic Church allow the ordination of women? How do we know God exists? How can we say that one religion is truer than another? Often the questions veer from topic to topic, with no connection among them and no effort on the part of the questioner to reach some ultimate goal. The person is not sure if his problem is with God, with organized religion, with a specific religion, or with all of it.

So, as you prepare for the journey, you must ask yourself: Where do the tensions lie? What is it that you seek? What do you want to know?

Examining Our Own Context

If we're going to search for God, if we're going to undertake the journey of discovery, we must examine the environments in which our questions take root—all the circumstances that shape our thinking about faith and that lead to conclusions about God and the world. We must identify these background theories and ask: What assumptions—about ourselves, God, and others—underlie our thinking? What are the hidden theories that determine our opinions about religion? Are we willing to change those theories? Are we willing to substitute those theories for new ones, depending upon what we discover? *Thank You*

When we examine our background theories, it doesn't mean we have to supersede our context entirely. As we will see later, God will work with us no matter who we are or where we live. If God wants to speak to us through Siri, he will. God can do so. But it does mean we must be aware of the ways we form judgments about things without ensuring these judgments have a well-founded basis.

Before we try to improve our spiritual health, we must investigate what impacts that health and what might cause our spiritual struggles in the first place. Every person must ask: What is my context? What do I want from the spiritual journey? What are the circumstances that shape my beliefs and assumptions? What is the intellectual and emotional "soil" in which my questions take root?

Why?

CHAPTER THREE

The Horizon of Uncertainty

To begin the journey of discovery with an open mind, we must recognize the assumptions and presuppositions that filter and shape our views of the world and of God. Assuming we have developed a receptive stance toward the life of faith, it's time to move forward. Within this twenty-first century culture, how do we journey from a wavering skepticism to confident belief? Let's begin by discussing a foundational fact of human existence: the horizon of uncertainty.

Of the dozens of students who rushed to Greg's bedside upon hearing news of his accident, most were seniors in high school. Because of this, they were in the midst of planning for graduation, for college, and perhaps for what they would study and where they might live. They were looking forward to the future with hope and a belief that the next phase of life would come about largely as they imagined.

Of course, no matter the age, we understand

where those students were coming from. We love to make plans. We plan for vacations, weddings, and birthdays, as well as for the minor events that fill our days. We schedule meetings and dinners, and we tell people we'll meet them for coffee or lunch.

In fact, most of us assume that the future will come about as we expect. We rarely impose conditions on plans or keep them tentative on the chance that something terrible will occur. When we plan to meet a friend for lunch, for example, we don't say, "I'll meet you at noon, provided that nothing happens to me while driving on the streets." If we lived with that mentality, society would break down; certainly our mental health would. We wouldn't plan anything—weddings, birthdays, or any of the little events that fill our days. We would diminish into a collective nervous wreck, afraid to commit to anything and living in constant fear. So we plan.

However, once we peer a little further into our plans, we find that underlying our hope and belief that things will go as we expect—that we will make it to retirement, that our kids will reach college, that we will attend next week's meeting—is the fact that *there is no certainty*.

No matter how much we plan, how much we install protocols, safety measures, contracts, or precautions, the future remains unknowable. Events remain outside our control. Consider the following three examples:

1. When you fall asleep, you don't worry that you will not wake up. But this is hardly because you can predict that you will. It's a scary thought, but a number of things could happen in the middle of the night that could end your life. An intruder could break in and harm you; a medical condition, previously undetected, could flare up. Or an earthquake could hit, a storm could roll through...the point is that when you fall asleep, you

cannot guarantee that you will wake up, or that you will do so uninjured. When you go to sleep at night, you enter a period of uncertainty and vulnerability.

2. When you drive to work, you may check your seatbelt, kick your tires, and focus on the road. But in spite of these precautions, you cannot be certain you will arrive to work safely. Glass on the road might slash and blow out your tire; the sun's glare might distract your eyes long enough for you to collide with the car in front of you; someone who is texting and driving might run a red light and strike your car.

3. Turning to a happier thought, consider the moment a woman tells a man, "I love you." That's a touching moment, but can the man be certain of it? Though she might say and do things that make it appear that she loves him, there is nothing she can do to make it absolutely certain. Even if she overwhelms him with gifts, she could still be doing it for the wrong reasons, for reasons that have nothing to do with love. There is no formula, either mathematically or otherwise, that tells us, once and for all, she loves him. There is no equation that gives us "love."

These are only a few examples, but the point in each is that there are significant stretches of our lives in which we cannot guarantee an event or condition. Even existence itself, our own being, remains mysterious. Can you guarantee that your heart will beat from one minute to the next? I'm not talking about likelihood. Of course it's likely. But are you *certain*? Can any of us be certain that we will be alive in an hour or even in thirty minutes? Although the odds favor our continued life, we possess no facts or knowledge that enable each of us to guarantee it.

The Paradox of Life

Reflecting upon this truth, we discover a fundamental feature of human existence, a background fact that applies to everyone at all times. Many authors and philosophers, including those in the Catholic tradition, have commented upon this feature that I call *the horizon of uncertainty.* The horizon of uncertainty is the sense of disruption and surprise that lurks within every moment, for good or bad. The horizon of uncertainty is the fundamental unpredictability of our present and future existence.

And yet, despite this uncertainty, we live and act as if matters and events are certain. We casually kiss our loved ones at night, assuming we will wake up the next morning. We brew the coffee with confidence that we will arrive to work on time. We dream as if we will attend college, marry, and play with our grandchildren. We save and invest on the assumption that there will come a time when we won't be working, when we descend into that final period of a long life known as retirement.

Why? Why do we prepare for the future despite the uncertainty that permeates every moment? Why do we fall asleep at night and make plans for the next day? If the courses of our lives are fundamentally uncertain, why do we live in many ways as though they are not?

At the heart of this paradox lies the essence of faith.

Reasons to Believe

In general, we live without fear of uncertainty because we have *reasons*, and if they are good reasons, we call them *credible*. Credible reasons are those that are trustworthy, well-founded, and legitimate. Credible reasons are the kinds of reasons that give the necessary assurance to move forward with a decision or plan of action.

So, why do we live as if what is fundamentally uncertain is certain? We live this way because when we consider all the relevant data, we have what amounts to a _credible reason to believe_. In other words, either explicitly or implicitly, expressed or unexpressed, we have concluded that, given all the relevant evidence, the hoped-for event or the anticipated outcome will materialize.

Consider again the three examples above:

1. _Waking up._ While I cannot be certain of waking up in the morning, the relevant facts and circumstances provide credible reasons to believe that I will. Currently, I have no serious health condition that might leave me incapacitated or dead during the night. My neighborhood is safe—it's not perfect, but safe. Plus, I lock my apartment doors and windows. In short, it seems unlikely that someone will break in and harm me.

   The same low probability holds for other possible threats. An earthquake, which is always a possibility in southern California, is not statistically likely to occur while I'm asleep, and even if it does, I will probably survive. The same goes for other potential calamities, like lightning, tornadoes, and hurricanes. And although I'm near an airport, the likelihood of a plane crashing into my home is low.

   A review of all the factors (what lawyers call the "totality of the circumstances") gives me good reasons to think that when I fall asleep at night, I will wake up the next morning. The reasons suggesting I will not wake up are either nonexistent or so unpersuasive as to be easily dismissed. I go to bed and plan for the next day, not because I have certainty, but because I have credible reasons to trust that all will be okay.

2. *Driving to work.* A similar analysis holds for my drive to work. A review of the credible reasons assures me that it's worth the risk. For example, I'm only driving on a few streets in a city that's not very populated; the roads are wide and well maintained; experience tells me that most drivers stop at red lights, that they drive the speed limit (or close to it), and that at 7:30 a.m. most people are cautious and sober. Moreover, weather conditions in my town almost never present any dangers. In short, I have credible reasons to believe I will arrive at work safely.

3. *The act or profession of love.* Finally, suppose a spouse or significant other says to you, "I love you." As I mentioned before, we cannot prove love like we can prove the temperature, but the vast majority of the time, we don't worry about love's lack of provability because the circumstances present us with credible reasons to believe. For example, the more I got to know my wife when we were dating, the more her actions could only be explained as self-sacrificing acts of love. She did things for me, seeking no return. She comforted me, she consoled me, she laughed with me, and she made it clear that my happiness was a priority. I had absolutely no reason to believe that her behavior was rooted in anything other than authentic affection. In short, she gave me credible reasons to believe that she was in love with me.

The Beginning of Faith

When we retreat from daily responsibilities and get some perspective on our lives, we see that virtually every moment is lived within the horizon of uncertainty, and we navigate this uncertainty by evaluating the circumstances that either furnish, or do not furnish, credible reasons for a commitment, belief, or way of action. Sometimes this evaluation is instantaneous; often, we are not conscious of working through the reasons. But the process is there nonetheless, and it is this balancing of the known and the unknown, with no evidence of certainty, that permeates our lives.

What does this mean? What are the consequences of recognizing this horizon? In each of these examples (falling asleep, driving to work, professing and accepting love) we make a basic act of *entrustment*: entrusting ourselves to a reality we cannot control, a reality we cannot master, a reality we cannot predict. We are entrusting ourselves to a possible future, a future that we are shaping according to our preferences.

In other words, we are entering a space of hope: living as if what we hope to come true will in fact come true, even though we can make no guarantees.[1] This is not blind hope or a reasonless entrustment, for we base our hope on credible reasons. But it remains an entrustment; an act of hope.

Once we recognize this, we start to understand what we mean by faith. In entering into lifelong commitments, in making plans for the future, in traveling, in entering into contracts, and in doing so much more throughout the course of our lives, we are making *acts of faith*. At its most basic level, faith is the act by which we entrust ourselves to unknown or uncertain realities because of the existence of credible reasons. This basic (nonreligious) faith, this foundational entrustment, is what makes life possible.

The Foundation of Faith

Faith is one of the foundations of our existence and flourishing. Like gravity, it is something we cannot see or hear, but it keeps us in psychological, spiritual, and emotional orbit. Without faith, we cannot live. Without daily acts of <u>entrustment,</u> we would not look forward to things and plan for the future. We wouldn't bother with school, for education depends upon the faith—the trust and reliance—we put in teachers, textbook publishers, scholars, coaches, and many others. Without some degree of faith, we wouldn't get on an airplane, for we must have faith that the pilots, the workers at the airport, and the security personnel have all gone through the proper training and have sufficiently performed their jobs.

Without faith, we'd expend enormous time and energy relearning and reteaching ourselves facts and truths that we otherwise believe. In the words of John Paul II:

> There are in the life of a human being many more truths which are simply believed than truths which are acquired by way of personal verification. Who, for instance, could assess critically the countless scientific findings upon which modern life is based? Who could personally examine the flow of information which comes day after day from all parts of the world and which is generally accepted as true? Who in the end could forge anew the paths of experience and thought which have yielded the treasures of human wisdom and religion? This means that the human being—the one who seeks the truth—is also *the one who lives by belief.*[2]

Though John Paul II uses the term *belief*, we can substitute the word *faith*. The human being is one who lives by faith, who lives by entrusting him- or herself.

This entrustment—this faith—holds even in an area that many assume to be free of faith: science. Even scientists entrust themselves and their work to conditions, realities, and laws they cannot fully prove or verify. Paul Davies, an astrophysicist at Arizona State University, wrote,

When I was a student, the laws of physics were regarded as completely off limits. The job of the scientist, we were told, is to discover the laws and apply them, not inquire into their provenance. The laws were treated as "given"—imprinted on the universe like a maker's mark at the moment of cosmic birth—and fixed forevermore. Therefore, to be a scientist, you had to have faith that the universe is governed by dependable, immutable, absolute, universal, mathematical laws of an unspecified origin. You've got to believe that these laws won't fail, that we won't wake up tomorrow to find heat flowing from cold to hot, or the speed of light changing by the hour.[3]

For Davies, the faith that scientists place in the laws of physics and chemistry mirrors the faith that people place in God and religion. According to Davies, "both religion and science are founded on faith—namely, on belief in the existence of something outside the universe, like an unexplained God or an unexplained set of physical laws, maybe even a huge ensemble of unseen universes, too." Consequently, "until science comes up with a testable theory of the laws of the universe, its claim to be free of faith is manifestly bogus."[4] Furthermore, Davies points out,

Just because the sun has risen every day of your life, there is no guarantee that it will therefore rise tomorrow. The belief that it will—that there are indeed dependable regularities of nature—is an act of faith, but one which is indispensable to the progress of science.[5]

What we noted earlier about credible reasons also applies in the context of science. Scientists don't possess a blind faith in the laws of science; rather, when they proceed with new experiments or test new hypotheses, they have credible reasons to trust that the physical constants or laws of nature—like the law of gravity, the speed of light, and the behavior of electrons—won't suddenly change. But these credible reasons still do not furnish a complete and total guarantee. Even scientists must trust in the data and the "stuff" of science. Even scientists live within the horizon of uncertainty. Even scientists, in the act of being scientists, possess faith.

Finally, consider the legal profession. In American criminal law, the standard for finding someone guilty of a crime is "beyond a reasonable doubt." This doesn't mean the jury has to remove all doubt whatsoever. This doesn't mean that the jury has to be 100 percent certain. In fact, that is rarely the case. Juries often convict people without complete certainty. But we don't worry about this because our legal system ensures that juries base their decisions on credible reasons, which they derive from the evidence. But this evidence can still be doubted, so the crucial element of trust is always present. The jury members must still trust that the lawyers have presented authentic evidence, that the prosecutor and the defense attorney have not joined in a conspiracy, and that the judge overseeing the case is competent and not corrupt. Similarly, the judge and lawyers have to trust that the jury members, too, are competent and not corrupt. In other words, a successful and fair judicial system requires a constant circle of faith.

In the Face of Uncertainty

Certainly, the preceding argument does not prove any particular religious faith. It doesn't mean that God exists. In fact, it hardly relates to God at all. At this stage, we have only established that our existence depends upon numerous acts of faith. We have to have faith because we cannot possibly verify or guarantee every event or condition upon which life depends. We live within a horizon of uncertainty.

In the face of this uncertainty, we turn to credible reasons that either do or do not furnish sufficient evidence to make a decision or engage in a certain act. In so doing, we entrust ourselves to realities that remain fundamentally uncertain, and we make an act of faith.

The question is not, Will I have faith? Or, Can I believe? But rather, In what do I believe and in what do I have faith? In other words, if faith is a natural part of being a human being, are there credible reasons for believing in the reality we call "God," and if so, what role does God have in our existence?

CHAPTER FOUR

The Nature of Being Human

It was to the horizon of uncertainty that my students and I became front row spectators as we gathered in grief outside Greg's hospital room. As the hours ticked on, we turned to a variety of ways of coping with unknowns. Some expressed hope in modern medicine; some gave up, assuming the worst to be inevitable; but a great many of us channeled our faith into both doctors and God. As a community anchored by a Catholic school, it was only natural. Asking for comfort, for healing, and for consolation, we tried to pray Greg to recovery.

The question of God is at the center of the 3 a.m. phone call and the horizon of uncertainty. The question of God is at the center of Christian life. What, then, are we to make of this most important and foundational question?

God's Existence

In using the term *God* here, we are not trying to advance a specific understanding of God; for example, that God is three in one or that God established a relationship with a particular group of people. Rather, we are referring to a notion of God that has some connection with the major world religions, but that also has roots in ancient philosophy—a notion of God as a source, being, or presence that transcends space and time, a "something" or "someone" that might be the cause of the known universe and might explain certain features and characteristics of the universe and everything in it (all of creation). What particular qualities this being has— whether it wants to communicate with us, whether our decisions matter, whether it is in the form of a human, and more—will be discussed in later chapters. At this point in our journey, having established that we have a natural faith by virtue of being human, we simply want to know whether there are credible reasons for extending this faith beyond what we can see, touch, or hear.

As we have already noted, all of life is lived within a horizon of uncertainty, and we respond to this uncertainty not by establishing absolute proof but by relying upon credible reasons that justify a belief, decision, or commitment. Based on this premise, we can dispense with the need to *prove* that God exists.

Within the history of Christianity, particularly Catholicism, a long intellectual tradition speaks of "proofs" of God's existence. Catholics sometimes hear about these proofs in connection with one of the great minds in world history, the thirteenth-century priest and scholar St. Thomas Aquinas, whose famous treatise, the *Summa Theologica* (Latin for "Summary of Theology"), offered five arguments for the existence of God. Aquinas referred to God having been "proved" in these five ways.

However, Aquinas does not mean *proved* as the modern person understands the word. The five ways of Aquinas are not attempts to show that God exists in the same way that I know my computer exists, or that I know two plus two equals four, as if God were observable by the senses or demonstrable through an equation. Rather, Aquinas was trying to show that the reasoning powers of the human mind, without the claims of a sacred text or divine revelation (for example, the Bible), could lead someone to believe in the being we call God. He was trying to show that the nature and structure of the universe and the nature and structure of the created world could only be explained by the existence of a cause that itself did not need to be caused—by the being we call God.

Today, people often get caught up in searching for "proof" in the contemporary twenty-first-century sense. Many Christians are now on the defensive, anxious to muster evidence that determines God's existence with as much certainty as the existence of the iPhone. Because of this burden, it is not uncommon to hear that people can't believe in God because there's no proof or that they cannot believe in God until someone proves he exists. What they seek is *incontrovertible evidence that reveals God's existence beyond a shadow of a doubt.*

What kind of proof would satisfy this burden is not clear, but regardless, this approach is doomed from the start. It creates an intellectual demand that people can never meet, and even if they did, it would almost certainly fail to satisfy.

Consider the example of Jesus' twelve apostles. The New Testament tells us that the apostles saw Jesus walk on water and feed five thousand people with only a few loaves of bread. They saw him heal those with paralysis and leprosy and bring the dead back to life.

If you're looking for evidence that God exists or that Jesus himself is God, you'd think you could do no better than what Jesus did. The apostles saw things that would probably make the typical person faint or rush to the eye doctor. And yet, even in the face of these miracles, these astonishing feats, the apostles struggled to believe. At one point in the Gospel of Mark, after the apostles have witnessed Jesus do things no human can do, Jesus predicts his death and resurrection. How do his followers react? Mark reports, "But they did not understand what he was saying and were afraid to ask him" (9:32). The Gospel of Mark also tells us that, when Mary Magdalene arrived to inform Jesus' followers of the Resurrection, the apostles were mourning and weeping (see 16:10)—mourning and weeping because, despite Jesus' predictions of his resurrection, the apostles were unsure he was coming back. They remained uncertain.

Many times throughout his ministry, Jesus rebukes his disciples for their lack of faith (cf. Matt 8:26). And many know the stories of Judas's betrayal and Peter's denial, two examples of how daily encounters with the miraculous don't necessarily provide immunity from weakness and unbelief.

In short, even though Jesus predicted he would rise after three days, even though his dazzling powers confirmed his extraordinary claims, the apostles *still* doubted. They still weren't sure what to make of Jesus. They still weren't sure that he was God. Their example reveals that even with seemingly unquestionable evidence, the mind still has the capacity to disbelieve, to wonder, and to question.

My students often say they will believe in God only if he does something obvious and unmistakable to make his existence evident. Some even say, without appreciating the irony, that he should come down from heaven and announce his presence. I remind them that that is precisely what Jesus did, and it wasn't enough. Jesus did what people apparently long for, and it got him killed.

There is a second reason why the desire to prove God's existence in the modern sense may not be as fruitful as people assume. For the sake of argument, imagine that an angel descended from heaven and told you something that revealed

36

God's existence with certainty. That would certainly be an amazing experience, but then what? Would this eliminate your problems? Would this revelation solve your questions about the human being, the nature of the universe, and the purpose of life? Of course it wouldn't.

Although knowing that God exists would likely provide some consolation, the angel's disclosure wouldn't tell you much else. What is God like? What does he expect from you? What does he expect from his creation? Is this a God who cares about what we do with our Sundays, or does he avoid day-to-day affairs? The answers to these questions would remain unknown unless God communicated a more detailed plan, unless God engaged in an ongoing disclosure of information.

Reflecting further, we know that mere knowledge of God's existence is not what we ultimately seek. For example, you know your parents exist, but this doesn't necessarily mean you and they enjoy a healthy relationship. It doesn't mean that you understand them or know what to expect from them, and vice versa. You want more. You want to spend time with them, laugh with them, share your highs and lows and mark the major moments of life together.

In other words, you seek conversation and affection. You seek communication and relationship. Merely knowing that your parents exist—or that your friends exist—doesn't provide much consolation unless your relationships with them include additional elements.

3. There is a third reason, among many, why we shouldn't be too anxious to prove God's existence. Again, suppose a messenger from heaven made it indisputably clear to you that God existed. If you told ten people about your experience, how many of them would believe you? Would everyone take you at your word, or would they deem you delusional, perhaps call you a liar? How would you convince them that the angel spoke to you?

What if they asked for evidence of the angel's existence? Could you give it to them?

Much of your audience, even your friends and family, would probably worry that something was wrong and doubt your claim. And what would you do in response? How would you persuade them? There is little you could do. You'd have to leave them with their disbelief and their whisperings about your sanity.

Consequently, the idea of asking for and receiving "proof" as understood in the modern sense is a difficult matter. Ultimately, it would probably deliver us none of the mental peace for which we had hoped.

This idea may be disappointing. You may wish that it was possible to reach a cruising altitude of certainty that would leave you free from the turbulence of doubt. While we cannot put that past God, the unlikelihood of reaching this certainty should not trouble you. To doubt, to wonder, and to question are actions of a healthy and liberated mind. They are part of the essence of our mental response to reality. To not doubt would require us to be something other than human.

Treat your capacity for questioning as a gift, not a liability, and don't let it impede your search for God. Our doubts and fears shouldn't cause debilitating guilt or worry. They should be honored as signs of vitality. We are not robots or puppets; we are human beings. The goal is not for us to overcome our questioning, but to integrate this capacity into our journey; to learn from mystery, not destroy it.

This is not to say that we should avoid asking if God exists or that we ought to believe in God blindly—just as our questions and our doubts don't make us abandon the pursuit of science or give up on finding love, two areas where mystery also exists. As we will note in future chapters and as Aquinas showed, there are very good reasons to believe in God. However, we should be careful not to invest the concept of certainty—absolute proof—with

more weight than it deserves, leading to inevitable disappointment once we realize that such certainty is not possible. It's
unlikely that we could ever obtain the foolproof evidence we
often think we need. And even if we could, would it be of much
use? In fact, it might make matters more difficult.

Therefore, in your quest to develop faith in God, begin with
a deep breath. We come to God with our vulnerability and the
limitations of our minds. We come to God with imperfect knowledge, and with confusions, doubts, and struggles. We come to
God within the horizon of uncertainty. This is the nature of being
human. Celebrate it!

CHAPTER FIVE

Faith in God

Having established that doubt and uncertainty are inherent in the journey of faith, we finally move to the heart of the matter—the question of God's existence. For anyone grappling with the demands of the 3 a.m. phone call, this is the question that has to be answered: Is there a Reality beyond this world, beyond every world, that hears our cries for help? In other words, can we believe in a being we call God?

We just noted that we don't have to take on the burden of proving God's existence beyond any doubt. So, for a rational, intelligent person, what makes God's existence not only possible, but likely? *What are the credible reasons that justify belief in the existence of God?*

While these questions may seem overwhelming, centuries of human experience and deep thinking reveal that having faith in God is not something that needs to happen randomly or without solid foundation. It is not something we have to leave up to chance, just hoping that at

40

some point we catch a wave of spirituality that will steer us to the shore of religious belief.

In other words, we don't journey without help. We can identify many ways that people throughout history have come to believe in God. These ways or "arguments"—what we have previously called credible reasons—provide us with evidence of a supernatural Reality, an existence that dwells in another dimension. Let us now explore some of these credible reasons for believing in God.

Personal Experience

Perhaps the most common way that God's existence becomes a possibility is through personal experience. For tens of thousands of years, people have undergone encounters that have led them to wonder, "Is there something, or someone, beyond the universe? Is there a force, perhaps a loving one, that oversees the day-to-day affairs of all that has been and all that will be created?"

In these moments, it's not necessarily the case that people "figure out" God or decide to practice a particular religion. Initially, people might not even associate this presence with God. They might feel more confusion than understanding. All they know is that something or someone has interrupted the typical patterns and expectations of this world. Something occurs that is truly *extra*ordinary, and it inspires people to move toward religious belief. — *existential*

The number and kind of experiences that fall into this category are as limitless and as varied as the number and kind of people. It might be one particular experience, but it could also be more than one. Some people, for example, detect the presence of a higher power in the beauty and magnificence of nature. A majestic landscape of snow-capped mountains or the vast silvery blue of a sunlit ocean might lead some to conclude there is no other explanation for such beauty than a heavenly presence, a Creator whose divine action has brought everything into being. Others might feel this presence in the joy of a birth or the excitement of a marriage. Such great happiness and love emerge that they seem to be a gift from a nonhuman dimension.

Some detect God in the surprising kindness of a stranger or a turn of luck too incredible to be explained as a coincidence. A few years ago, while driving a group of students to a mock trial competition, we stopped at a red light. Without any cars in front of me, I was planning to turn left. While waiting for the light to turn green, my thoughts turned to the precious souls in the vehicle, how much their parents love them, and the importance of being responsible and cautious. The magnitude of my responsibility was an overwhelming feeling that brought peace.

When the red light changed to a green arrow, I felt the need to pause and look both ways, one more time, just in case I had missed something. Suddenly, a car raced through the intersection, running a red light. Had I not waited, our vehicle would have been hit and there would have been a major accident.

Why did I feel compelled to pause before accelerating on that day, when I had not done so on other occasions? What gave me that extra sense? Why did I have such peace and alertness? Although I already believed in God, that moment left me in speechless awe, strengthening my belief that a Greater Intelligence oversees our lives.

Where, in your life, have you experienced something too mysterious or too incredible to be explained on human terms? Where have you felt or sensed a Reality or Intelligence beyond this world? What was different about that experience? What made it *extra*ordinary?

Objective Credible Reasons

Sensing God in personal experience is common, but these encounters are generally so personal and so tied to particular circumstances they are hard to communicate. A personal experience, even something as dramatic as a vision, can fade into the endless inbox of daily encounters, and we often recall these experiences no better than a stranger we once passed in the street.

Fortunately, there are other experiences that draw people to the idea of God, experiences that are more objective in nature and dependent on information available to everyone. This information, or evidence, provides reasons for believing in a supernatural existence or Reality that we call God.

Consider the criminal justice system and how prosecutors gather evidence. After a crime, the perpetrator is often not obvious. Suspects don't usually admit guilt or surrender. Consequently, police gather evidence, and the prosecutor works with the police to decide what the evidence suggests about the identity of the perpetrator. For example, suppose someone breaks into a vehicle and steals someone's wallet from the center console. Suppose the police and prosecutors arrive at the scene of the crime and observe the broken window, along with blood on the front seat and a few strands of hair.

Without any direct evidence of the burglary—for example, a hidden camera that clearly shows the face of the perpetrator—prosecutors and police must analyze the clues, the hair and the blood, to determine the suspect. The clues act as a kind of "signature." If police run a DNA test on the hair and the blood and the results point to one person, the police now have a lead. They have evidence of who may have committed the crime.

However, even if the hair and blood tests point to one specific person, this doesn't mean that this person broke into the car. There remains the slight possibility that he or she was framed. The prosecutor and police will have to make that determination. They will visit the suspect. If they do, and they notice a cut on his hand consistent with someone who broke a car window, it becomes even more likely that this suspect is the actual perpetrator.

In the American justice system, lawyers don't always work with direct evidence of a crime or illegal action. Juries and judges have to weigh clues, evidence, bits and pieces of information that explain the circumstances found at the crime scene. Based on the evidence, lawyers craft a story about what happened. Then they ask juries to believe that story. Juries convict or acquit people based on the evidence.

The above example helps us understand how we can believe that God exists even if some doubt remains, even if we don't have direct evidence of God. Most humans will not have an unfiltered or unmediated encounter with God. However, this doesn't mean we are left blind. As in police work, we can conclude that a supernatural Reality exists based on the evidence that is available to our minds and our senses through a reflection upon the created world. In other words, a belief in God arises not because of wishful thinking or blind belief, but because there is no better explanation for what we observe to be true about the world. We can point to certain circumstances that strongly indicate that a supernatural Reality exists. As in the case of criminal law, the lack of direct evidence is not a problem.

What is this evidence or the credible reasons for believing that God exists? Let us now examine some logical explanations that lead us toward the belief in God that many in the Christian tradition have found persuasive. The reasons are not exhaustive, nor are they meant to remove all doubt. Belief in God is less a matter of securing perfect evidence than of the mind and heart moving in a general direction, developing a basic orientation toward reality.

The Idea of Intelligibility

One path to God that is more objective in nature arises from a feature that every person can observe about the universe—what philosophers and theologians call the universe's *intelligibility*, or the idea that the universe is "figure-out-able."

In other words, the universe possesses order and logic. It is knowable and understandable, not haphazard and random. The study of the sciences and mathematics discloses a world that contains rationality to its very core.

Consider, for example, the field of medicine. The profession of medicine exists because the body and its functions—how it works and how it heals—can be discovered and regulated. If you tear your knee ligaments, the doctors can repair them because the "stuff" of the problem—the skin, the ligaments, the blood flow, and more—work according to physical, chemical, and biological laws. In the language of philosophy, the body is "intelligible"; that is, it is comprehensible. It has an inherent capacity to be known and figured out, and this capacity enables doctors and scientists to understand it and make reliable decisions.[1]

The same intelligibility, the same "figure-out-ability," is present in countless other areas of our universe and permits us to have a meaningful, coherent existence. We can fly airplanes, send astronauts to the moon, make phone calls, drive cars, listen to music, send emails, receive vaccines, and more because the natural world, at the physical, chemical, and biological levels, possesses a system of laws and internal processes that don't change. These laws, in fact, work together, as if they were all part of a master plan.

The natural world, in short, can be figured out. The study of nature discloses a set of instructions for how to shape, harness, and manage nature. In a word, nature is *intelligible*.[2]

Now, this order and intelligibility relate to the question of God because they necessarily raise questions: What is the basis for this intelligibility? How is it that the universe contains such order, such predictability, such comprehensibility and rationality? Why does the universe seem to bear the reflection of an intelligent mind?

Consequently, we're left with two choices: either this intelligibility is the product of mere chance, or it is the product of a mind that intended it. Though many say this quality of intelligibility just happened by chance—that it's simply one of the unplanned aftereffects of the Big Bang—it is a poor explanation.

The intelligibility in the universe cannot be derived from a non-intelligible source, for that would be like saying a full glass of water came from another glass that was empty. Something cannot give what it does not possess. If non-intelligibility—no God, no creator, no intelligent mind—is at the source of everything that exists, then this absolute randomness could not produce the intelligible realities that we experience every day. Moreover, if all that exists truly came from a non-intelligible source, we would be incapable of knowing it anyway because the human mind itself would be the product of this non-intelligibility, and therefore it would be unable to make reliable judgments about the world in which it exists.[3]

The better explanation lies elsewhere. If the universe seems to be run by an unseen set of laws, the best explanation is that there is a supreme lawgiver. If the physical and natural world appears to be governed by systems and processes that coordinate with one another, the more likely explanation is that there was an intelligent Reality that arranged the coordination. In other words, this is a being, or Reality, with the capability of exercising intention and implementing a master plan. More simply, if the world seems to possess clues that direct us toward a larger whole, the more likely explanation is that there is a clue-giver. Whether we call that entity a lawgiver, a clue-giver, the source of intelligibility, or something else, it is this kind of being that we associate with the existence of God.

The Evidence of Design

Related to the evidence of intelligibility is the evidence of design. To understand how the evidence of design in the world relates to God's existence, imagine the following scenario.

Suppose you're driving in the middle of nowhere. There are no roads, and you often have to swerve to avoid rocks, nails, tree stumps, and gooey puddles of water. Trash blows aimlessly and stray animals sniff for food. In the distance, you see what looks like a toilet, but it's corked in the mud, half broken.

You keep driving, and eventually the rough gravel gives way to smoothly paved roads. A sign says, "Welcome to Townville." Instead of a wild mixture of plants, flowers, and trees, the grounds have been cut and trimmed and neatly arranged. There are special places to deposit waste and trash. The farther you go, the more roads you start to see. Shops, stores, clinics, and restaurants surround a grid of perpendicular streets. There are lights and signs signaling when people should stop and when they should go.

Now compare these two different landscapes: the one that is wild and unpaved and the one that is paved and ordered. One of the obvious differences is that the latter contains evidence of being designed. It seems to have people and their needs in mind. Things are in their proper places. The natural landscape has been altered for the specific purpose of accommodating people who need to move, eat, buy necessities, and use the bathroom, and who need to do so safely. The signs indicate when cars have the right of way and when pedestrians do. Trash and waste are disposed of properly so that the neighborhood is healthy, clean, and beautiful. There are also places to go if people hurt themselves.

In other words, the evidence indicates that Townville has been planned. There is evidence of coordination, intention, and anticipation. If someone said that this community—the community of the paved streets, the stoplights, the stores, and everything else—came about randomly; that the wind, for example, happened to blow through the natural landscape in such a way as to pull together bricks and boards and nails to create the community, you'd find it absurd. It would be impossible—or as close to impossible as it gets—for nature to produce Townville without assistance from minds that could intentionally construct it.

The more credible explanation is that the community and the buildings came about because a group of people conceived Townville in their imagination and then constructed their plan. The underlying principle is that if there is evidence of design, there is likely a designer. If there is evidence of intention, there is likely someone who has done the intending.

The universe is like Townville but on a much larger scale: it possesses evidence of design, and the logical explanation is that there was a master designer. Because of the vastness and complexity of the universe, this designer must be quite an extraordinary being, someone or something that infinitely surpasses human capabilities. In other words, this being must possess a magnitude, an excellence, and an intelligence that we normally associate with a Creator, with the kind of Reality that people associate with God.

What's the evidence for this design? It's everywhere. Everywhere we look, we see evidence of coordination, planning, and intention. Consider the human body. In the circulatory system, for example, the heart works with the lungs to pump blood throughout the body, providing oxygen, water, and nutrients to our cells and ensuring that our bodies maintain homeostasis.

Each part works in harmony with the others. When we run, our heart speeds up to pump more blood because the brain sends signals to indicate that the body needs more oxygen. When our blood pressure changes too dramatically, the body's systems kick in to restore balance. We don't do a thing; it just happens. Have you ever wondered why?

What explains such extraordinary complexity, sophistication, and coordination? How is it that the heart knows to interact with the lungs, and how and why do both of them work together day after day, hour after hour, to ensure our survival and health? How does the brain know what to do? What explains the extraordinary capacities of the brain to direct the infinitely complex interactions of the body?[4]

Again, we're left with a choice: either these remarkable features came from a non-intelligible and incomprehensible source, or they came about at the direction of a being who purposely arranged the chemical and physical interactions to be what they are and do what they do. Like the streets and stoplights in the fictional Townville, the various components of the chemical and biological world, all of which seem to coordinate with each other like a finely tuned piece of music, do not appear to be the result of arbitrary and mindless interactions. Rather, they appear to reflect a mind—a composer of creation—that has orchestrated things to be what they are. What do we call this master composer? Such an entity goes by many names, one of which is God.

The Origin of Life

Connected to the evidence of design and the idea of intelligibility are the facts involving the origin of all life. One of the most increasingly popular reasons for raising the possibility of God is the astonishing things we are learning about the *remarkable* unlikelihood of the emergence of organic life. Essentially, the coming into being of an *anthropic* universe—a universe capable of life, particularly human life—is so incomprehensibly improbable, so unfathomably unlikely, that it suggests that a supernatural source (God) intended for such life to come about. To appreciate the significance of this, some background information will be helpful.

It is scientific fact that the existence of human and nonhuman life depends upon certain conditions and laws that scientists call "constants." These constants "fix the parameters of interaction and interrelationship among space, time, and different kinds and emissions of energy. They therefore have very precise values in all places and times."[5] Examples of these constants include: "the speed of light constant, Planck's constant, the gravitational constant, weak force constant, strong force constant, mass of a proton, mass of an electron, charge of an electron/proton, etc."[6] If these conditions, or constants, were different by the *tiniest* of amounts, life on earth would not have been possible.

The best way to understand this path to God is to review some of the data. Ian Barbour, for example, drew on the work of Albert Einstein to discuss the significance of the expansion rate following the Big Bang. Barbour wrote,

> Stephen Hawking writes, "If the rate of expansion one second after the Big Bang had been smaller by even one part in a hundred thousand million million, it would have recollapsed before it reached its present size." On the other hand, if it had been greater by a part in a million, the universe would have expanded too rapidly for stars and planets to form.[7]

Scholars at the Biologos Foundation have noted the significance of the density of the universe at the time of the Big Bang:

> The precision of density must have been so great that a change of one part in 10^{15} (i.e. 0.0000000000001%)

would have resulted in a collapse, or big crunch, occur-
ring far too early for life to have developed, or there
would have been an expansion so rapid that no stars,
galaxies or life could have formed. This degree of precision would be like a blindfolded man choosing a single
lucky penny in a pile large enough to pay off the United
States' national debt.[8]

Consider the strength of gravity and this extraordinary fact:
"if we change gravity by even a tiny fraction of a percent—enough
so that you would be, say, one billionth of a gram heavier or
lighter—the universe becomes so different that there are no stars,
galaxies, or planets. And without planets there would be no life."[9]

Barbour described additional evidence of this "fine-tuning":

If the strong nuclear force were even slightly weaker we
would have only hydrogen in the universe. If the force
were even slightly stronger, all the hydrogen would
have been converted to helium. In either case, stable
stars and compounds such as water could not have
been formed. Again, the nuclear force is only barely
sufficient for carbon to form; yet if it had been slightly
stronger, the carbon would have all been converted
into oxygen. Particular elements, such as carbon, have
many other special properties that are crucial to the
later development of organic life as we know it.[10]

Barbour says that one "could list other unexplained 'remarkable
coincidences,' such as the fact that the universe is homogenous and
isotropic."[11] Essentially, "the simultaneous occurrence of many
independent improbable features appears wildly improbable."[12]

A number of well-known scientists and theologians have
concluded that, given (a) the extraordinary improbability of the
conditions necessary for life; and (b) the fact that life did in fact
come about, then (c) some sort of intelligent Reality must have
intended the universe to bring forth life. In other words, if the

constants and conditions necessary for the existence of life are so unlikely and depend upon such minute and exact parameters, it seems plausible that something must have created the constants to be what they are. It seems *exceedingly* unlikely that these conditions came about by pure chance.

The Jesuit Robert Spitzer, SJ, has said that the likelihood of these constants emerging by pure chance, by simply the unplanned and random interaction of the primordial material left over from the Big Bang, can be compared to the likelihood of a monkey sitting in front of a typewriter and happening to type out, · without help, the entire text of *Hamlet*.

In other words, the nature of the physical and material world appears to have been fine-tuned to produce life, and this evidence of "fine tuning could be taken as an argument for the existence of a designer, perhaps a God with an interest in conscious life."[13]

The Moral Law

A fifth feature of the world that many say points to the likelihood of a supernatural being (that is, God) is the presence of the moral law. Indeed, this is one of the most prominent reasons why people argue for the existence of a God.

Moral law is the sense of right and wrong to which all human beings feel obligated. Across all cultures and times, there are standards of justice and injustice, of actions and behaviors that are either permitted or not permitted.

This doesn't mean that everyone agrees on what is right and wrong. This can vary drastically among different human groups. But despite differences about precise applications of what is right and wrong, people still agree that some actions are right and others are wrong.[14]

As with the above evidence, the persistence of moral law raises the question: Where does this internal sense come from? How is it that human beings have this deeply impressed belief that they ought to act a certain way, that they must uphold standards of behavior even when it is very difficult, even when it goes against their own interests?

The answer has to do with God. Many people have proposed that the reason there is a universal belief in a standard of right and wrong is that there is an intelligent Reality that has impressed such a belief upon us. In other words, if there is a moral law, there must be a lawgiver. The name for this lawgiver is *God*.

An Outside Reality

The above outline is not exhaustive, and for each of the reasons, there are nuances, variations, and objections. If the subject of God's existence were a vast museum, we have seen only a few paintings. Moreover, nothing stated so far proves God's existence or *guarantees* that there is a supernatural Reality. Remember: we're just talking about evidence, about clues, about signs. We don't have foolproof data.

My aim has been more limited but still very important: to persuade you to continue further into the museum; to show, in other words, how and why the faith that we naturally have as human beings, as discussed in chapter 3, might begin to extend to a Reality outside of space and time, to a Reality that we call *God*.

Consequently, the above evidence can open us to the possibility and even likelihood of God's existence. What kind of God this might be and what that God might expect of us will be explored in later chapters. For now, the evidence simply suggests that some kind of outside Reality, some kind of Intelligent Presence, is required for our own existence and that of the universe.

FRANCIS COLLINS

Let's now explore how the explanations noted above can coalesce into the layers of a person's life; how they can impact the spiritual journey of a pilgrim in search of truth.

For many people, there isn't one particular path to God above all else. It's not usually the case that someone reads about the moral law or the design inherent within nature and suddenly decides to believe in God. Usually, it's more complicated and requires a range of encounters and experiences over time. For many, the path to God combines the different paths we spoke of above. One of my favorite examples of this kind of encounter with God is the story of world-famous scientist and doctor Francis Collins.

Collins is known worldwide not only for his scientific achievements but also for his efforts to integrate science and religion. He is the former Director for the National Institutes of Health, and he also led the effort to decode the human genome. In addition to his groundbreaking scientific work, he has tried to show how one can believe both in the scientific understanding of the world and in the Christian faith.[15]

Collins, however, did not always believe in God. He grew up in the Christian religion as a member of the Episcopal Church, but it never took hold. As a boy, he sang in a church choir, but he never developed a consistent religious practice. Later, he went to study quantum mechanics at Yale, where he became "compelled with the notion that everything in the universe [could] be described in a second-order differential equation."[16] He thought mathematics and physics could answer the great questions of life, and the more he studied, the more his faith dwindled. As Collins tells it, "I concluded that all of this stuff about religion and faith was a carryover from an earlier, irrational time, and now that

54

science had begun to figure out how things really work, we didn't need it any more."[17]

After receiving his doctorate, Collins decided to attend medical school. Due to the encounters he had with his patients, he began to reconsider God's existence and the life of faith:

> Some of my patients were clearly relying very heavily on their faith as a source of strength in circumstances that were pretty awful. They had terrible diseases from which they were probably not going to escape, and yet instead of railing at God, they seemed to lean on their faith as a source of great comfort and reassurance. They weren't, somehow, perceiving it as the really awful thing that it seemed to me to be. And that was interesting and puzzling and unsettling.[18]

Surprised at the hope his patients placed in God despite their illnesses, Collins wanted to know more. He realized that he had rejected God and religious belief based on reasons similar to those we discussed in chapter 2. He possessed unexamined background theories that ruled out God from the start: "I had made a decision to reject any faith view of the world without ever really knowing what it was that I had rejected."[19]

Collins became uncomfortable with his own assumptions about religion and wanted to know what motivated his patients. In discussing the nature of the Christian faith with Collins, a Methodist minister gave him a copy of C. S. Lewis's famous book *Mere Christianity*. For Collins, this wasn't simply a book; it was a doorway into a new dimension.

While reading *Mere Christianity*, Collins discovered that people could believe in God not because of wishful thinking or mere superstition, but because they had critically reflected upon the nature of the world. Collins started to accept that believing in God was actually more rational than not believing in God. In his reading and through his searching, Collins found credible reasons for God's existence.

One of the arguments that most compelled Collins was the presence of the moral law. For him, this was not only evidence of a God, but crucially, of a loving God:

> Where did [the moral law] come from? I reject the idea that that is an evolutionary consequence, because that moral law sometimes tells us that the right thing to do is very self-destructive. If I'm walking down the river-bank, and a man is drowning, even if I don't know how to swim very well, I feel this urge that the right thing to do is to try to save that person. Evolution would tell me exactly the opposite: preserve your DNA. Who cares about the guy who's drowning? He's one of the weaker ones, let him go. It's your DNA that needs to survive. And yet that's not what's written within me.
>
> Lewis argues that if you are looking for evidence of a God who cares about us as individuals, where could you more likely look than within your own heart at this very simple concept of what's right and what's wrong. And there it is. Not only does it tell you something about the fact that there is a spiritual nature that is somehow written within our hearts, but it also tells you something about the nature of God himself, which is that he is a good and holy God. What we have there is a glimpse of what he stands for.[20]

However, Lewis's arguments for God's existence alone were not sufficient to enable Collins to assent to a belief in God. Though Lewis's book nudged him in the direction of belief, inclined him to be open to God's existence, and made the idea of God a very real possibility, Collins wasn't ready to declare his faith. "Intellectual argument," he said, had pushed him to the "precipice of belief," but he needed something else to get him across the gap, to help him fully and finally proclaim a belief in God. That "something" was a personal experience:

> I struggled with [belief] for many months, really resisting this decision, going forward, going backward. Finally, after about a year, I was on a trip to the northwest, and on a beautiful afternoon hiking in the Cascade Mountains, where the remarkable beauty of the creation around me was so overwhelming, I felt, "I cannot resist this another moment. This is something I have really longed for all my life without realizing it, and now I've got the chance to say yes." So I said yes. I was 27. I've never turned back. That was the most significant moment in my life.[21]

The story of Francis Collins helps us understand the way that many paths can intertwine in a person's life. Intellectual argument—reflecting upon the moral law, for example—could only take Collins a certain distance. It was helpful and persuasive, but it wasn't enough. Something more personal and more mysterious needed to happen for him to conclude, with his whole being, that God existed. Collins couldn't argue his way into faith. He had to be patient enough to let God make a move.

Consequently, we cannot calculate how and when a person will come to take an interest in God. Pope Benedict XVI once said there are as many paths to God as there are people. He's right. Every person comes to God on a different timeline. Some find God's existence a relatively simple matter, other people take years to work through the question, and some, of course, remain permanently uncertain, unable to commit either way.

However, we are not left clueless. We are not left to gaze at the sky without any signs pointing the way. When we reflect upon the universe, we observe certain features and patterns that seem to be explained only by a supernatural Reality. In addition, people of every generation report experiences and encounters that indicate the presence of this same Reality, a force or being that cannot be explained on purely human terms. It is on this basis, and not on the basis of mere wishful thinking, that we can begin to develop a faith in God.

CHAPTER SIX

God's Revelation

Even if we are still unsure about many areas of religion and faith, we have made great progress in stepping outside our own minds to examine our assumptions and background theories concerning these subjects. We know that we exist within a horizon of uncertainty and that we are constantly called to believe, to have faith, and to entrust— not blindly, but based on credible reasons.

Furthermore, even if we don't yet believe in the being we call "God," we have solid reasons to believe in the existence of a Reality beyond space and time, beyond this dimension. In the journey of faith, each of us advances at our own pace. Give yourself credit for getting this far.

From Divine Reality to Personal God

In the last chapter, we identified credible reasons for God's existence. This information is no

small achievement, but on its own, it is of limited value. We need details and specifics. For example, does God care about us? Does he listen to our prayers? Does he help us in times of trouble?

My students and colleagues who joined in sorrow near Greg's hospital room yearned for a relationship with God, not mere knowledge of his existence. They wanted to know that God had heard their appeals. Appreciating something as abstract as the intelligibility of the universe or the universality of the moral law wasn't going to tell them if this Force, this Person, or this Reality might save Greg's life.

Similarly for most of us, once we have established credible reasons to extend our faith beyond the things of this world, we wonder whether it's possible to enjoy some ongoing relationship with the intelligent Reality who is the source of existence in the first place. Is this Reality interested in our lives and our concerns? Does it protect us from danger or assist us when we are in trouble?

Raising these questions presents a challenge. On our own, we cannot discover the answers. Human reason—the human capacity to reflect upon, analyze, and understand the world; our capacity to be aware of our own thoughts—reaches a limit. Suppose, for example, we want to know if God has a plan for us, whether he cares about what we do with our Sundays, or whether he calls each person to a particular role or career. Suppose we want to know if there is a dimension beyond this world, what Christians call "heaven." We could discuss these questions and hypothesize without end, but if God himself never weighed in, we would never know. At some point, God has to step out of the shadow of mystery and reveal himself.

Fr. Robert Barron has compared the stages of coming to know about God with the stages of coming to know another person.[1] In today's world, for example, if a man wants to learn more about a woman, he might Google her name. This Google search would probably yield useful details. The man might discover where the woman lives, where she works, and where she attended school. This man might know a few of her friends and ask them about her. Based on these initial investigations, he could probably discover good information.

However, to really know who this woman is—what she likes and dislikes, what she longs for and cherishes, what she fears and what she dreams about—this man will have to meet this woman, and she will have to reveal her feelings to him. She will have to tell him things that only she could know and articulate. She will have to talk about her past and her family and give context for understanding her opinions and worldview. Until she does this, the man's knowledge remains restricted to what he might find on Google or through talking to her acquaintances and friends.

At that point, notes Fr. Barron, the man faces a choice. Will he trust her? Will he believe what she says? When it comes to this woman's interior life, this man will no longer be able to objectively verify what she says. If she says she dreams about becoming an artist or that she is struggling to believe in God, he has to decide whether to trust what she says.

A similar dynamic, according to Fr. Barron, exists with God. With God, we can do our research and arrive at some preliminary conclusions concerning his existence. But we won't know intimate details unless God chooses to reveal himself, unless God chooses, in some way, to communicate with us. And at that point, we face a choice: Will we trust him?

Christians believe this is precisely what happened. Christians believe that God stepped out of his infinite mystery to reveal himself; not fully and completely, not to the point where humans know everything, but in important ways, Christians believe God has made himself known.

Does It Matter?

At this point, my students often raise the question: Does it matter? In other words, why should someone care about connecting with God? Why do we have to think about whether God has made himself known?

First, in Catholic teaching, God is the creator of everything that exists. God is not one being among many others; rather, he is *being itself*. God is the explanation for everything else's existence. God makes every other existence possible.

Assuming God exists, for humans to discover how to live optimally, the best thing we can do is communicate with our Creator. The following analogy might be helpful: the space shuttles that carry astronauts to outer space are some of the most sophisticated machines ever constructed. If you want to know how these machines work and why certain parts do what they do, the place to start is with the scientists and engineers who designed and built them or with someone who has been trained by the scientists and engineers.

Our situation before God is the same. If we want to know how to flourish, if we want to know the nature and purpose of our lives, the place to start is with the being who created us. God is the engineer who made all of creation, which includes all the physical, chemical, and natural laws that govern it. God alone can give us the roadmap for happiness and success.

Therefore, if we discovered that God spoke to humans, it would be to our immense advantage to know what he said. Moreover, if we learned that this Divine Reality wanted to create a relationship and that he wanted to communicate with us about our lives and concerns, we would have even more reasons to make this inquiry. This relationship could alter the course of our lives in fundamental, wonderful ways, perhaps even affecting our condition or state beyond this earth, after death.

The Bible as God's Word

Christians believe that the Creator has established a relationship and begun communication with human beings. How do we know God has done this? Where do we find the details of God's self-disclosure?

Christians believe that God has revealed himself to certain groups of people and that these people, through the centuries, have recorded his thoughts in a collection of writings. This collection of writings, or books, is what the world knows as the Bible.[2]

Mindful of our background theories, we must approach the Bible with an open, curious, and patient mind. It is a rich and fascinating collection of books that span many genres, cultures, languages, and historical periods. Unfortunately, disputes over specific passages or interpretations tend to distract people from the Bible's essential meanings. People hear about a man being swallowed by a whale (Jonah), about men walking on water (Jesus or Peter), or about God parting a sea, and they conclude the Bible is full of bizarre tales that cannot speak to the modern scientific mind.

In many cases, however, the people who make these judgments, though well meaning, have not studied the Bible in depth. They base their opinions on fragments they read as a child or on the underinformed comments of others. To appreciate the Bible more fully, we must not only carefully read the individual passages but also spend time studying the broader context within which the stories and books were written.

Consider, for example, the perspective of a physician, scientist, and professor at the University of Chicago, Leon Kass, who had long assumed that the Bible was "not...a book carefully constructed or worth studying as closely as the works of the great philosophers or poets."[3] He thought it was "an edifying book that spoke only to believers." One day, he listened to a fellow professor from the University of Chicago discuss the intricacies of the book of Genesis. As Kass reflected on this conversation, he said, "I realized that I had badly underestimated the subtlety of the [Bible] and that I had yet to learn how to read it."[4] Inspired by the encounter, Kass began weekly readings of the Bible and noted the effect of this reading:

> The stories of Genesis took hold of me. Though the characters seemed larger than life, the troubles they faced were clearly not so different from our own. I brought the stories to the family dinner table, where conversation was keen but closure was never reached about their meaning. There was, it seemed evident, deep wisdom to be found here, but it would not be available without great effort. I knew I had to persist.[5]

Kass persisted, and eventually began teaching a course on the Bible at the University of Chicago, eventually writing an entire book on the Book of Genesis. Kass's change in perspective testifies to how an open, curious mind can unlock the treasures of the biblical texts.

God's Self-Expression

While the Bible is indeed a work of literature, the Catholic Church discerns more than human influence in the text, referring to it as the inspired "word of God." Through the stories and books of the Bible, or Sacred Scripture, God speaks to humans. In the words of Pope Benedict XVI, the Bible "speaks to us of the inner life of God."[6]

The term that describes God's self-communication is *revelation*. The Bible is the record of God *revealing* himself to human beings. This doesn't mean God dropped the pages from heaven, leaving humans to collect and collate the pages into a book. Nor do Christians believe that the Bible is the result of some kind of dictation, as if the human authors were listening to God's voice and transcribing his words. Instead, in the words of Carey Walsh, God's revelation:

> ...is best understood as a dynamic process involving centuries of oral storytelling, written sources, later editing, copying in scrolls, and, finally, the communal determination of what constitutes the canon—the authoritative texts deemed holy—of sacred writings....
>
> The entire process, from God's self-communication in some manner to oral sharing to the transmission and collection of materials over centuries, comprises revelation. It presumes that all the unnamed people involved in producing the scrolls discerned holy presence in events and in transmitting written materials.[7]

With God as the primary author, Christians believe that God inspired the human authors of the Bible—that God moved the hearts and minds of the biblical authors to record God's revelation. Through these human "instrumental authors," God communicated his plan. However, God didn't treat the human authors as puppets or robots. The humanity of the authors, with their flaws, prejudices, and inaccuracies, remains present.

Despite this human element, Christians believe God's message shines through. Think of blinds covering a window, and imagine they are drawn partially open. Though the blinds will obscure much of the outside world, rays of light find their way through the cracks to illuminate the inside of the room. In connection with the Bible, think of the humanity of the authors—all their failings and prejudices, their limited perspectives and historical shortcomings—as the blinds, and consider the light to be the content of the divine messages. Despite the mistakes and misjudgments of the authors, the light of God's self-revelation finds a way to reach the reader. God trusts the humans, even though they aren't perfect, to convey his messages.

The Bible Is Inspired

Many people struggle with the divine origin of the Bible, believing that God no more inspired the Bible than he did the works of Mark Twain. That's an understandable reaction. The doctrine of biblical inspiration is an audacious, stunning claim. It *should* catch us off guard. I'd be worried if someone were not astonished by this, even skeptical. Indeed, there is a long line of biblical figures who had to reconfigure their typical understanding of reality to accommodate the divine plan.

While incomprehension is not necessarily a problem, we are still left with questions: How does God work through the authors? How do we know they communicated God's Word?

Unfortunately, no test or formula can demonstrate conclusively that the Bible is the result of God's inspiration. The doctrine of biblical inspiration remains a great mystery. We can, however, point to certain reasons that give direction. For example: St. Paul considered the Old Testament (the Hebrew Scriptures) to be inspired by God. He wrote, "All Scripture [referring to the Hebrew Scriptures] is inspired by God and is useful for teaching, for reproof, for correction, and for training in righteousness" (2 Tim 3:16–17). Jesus Christ, whom Christians believe to be God in the flesh, quoted the Hebrew Scriptures often and treated those writings as the Word of God. And the Catholic Church, which Catholics believe to be preserved from error in regards to faith and morals, confirms that the Old and New Testaments are divinely inspired.

Much more can be said on the topic, as it is vast, complex, and susceptible to different interpretations. Ultimately, no matter how much we read, we will still have questions: <u>How</u> can we trust St. Paul? <u>How</u> can we trust Jesus? <u>How</u> can we trust the Catholic Church?

To understand the bold claim of scriptural inspiration, it is necessary to read and study the biblical texts themselves. Be drawn into the stories and characters, and consult a commentary to help you unfold the richness of the language, the allusions, and the insights into humanity. Do this as much as you can with every aspect of the Bible. Stay open, curious, and engaged.

For centuries, these texts have nourished people's lives, giving them guidance, consolation, and wisdom. It's not just a small group of people who believe the Bible to be inspired; countless people across all parts of the world have found in the scriptures an inexhaustible divine treasure, words that challenge, provoke, inspire, and transform. No text, not even the plays of Shakespeare or the works of the great Greek philosophers, rivals what the Bible has done for so many people for so long.

Like all things involving God, the Bible is a mystery that has to be personally experienced to be appreciated. Like any mystery, biblical inspiration invites our faith, even in the midst of uncertainty and risk.

The Old and New Testaments

Christians divide the Bible into two main sections: the Old Testament (also known as the Hebrew Scriptures) and the New Testament.[8] The Old Testament tells the story of God's call of, and unfolding relationship with, the Hebrew people, later known as the Israelites or Jews. For Christians, the New Testament fulfills and completes the Old Testament and tells the story of Jesus Christ.

Although a thorough overview of the Bible goes far beyond

the scope of this work, a few elements of the Old Testament are worth noting.

The Old Testament tells the story of a relationship—the relationship between God and the Hebrews. This relationship begins with the call of a man named Abraham, with whom God forms a covenant (a covenant involves the exchange of promises between two parties). God promises Abraham descendants and blessings in exchange for Abraham's faithfulness. Abraham and his wife, Sarah, previously childless, are blessed with children, and their children have children, and eventually one of their grandsons—Jacob—is renamed "Israel" by an angel of the Lord. Because of that renaming, Jacob's descendants are known as the "Israelites" (later they will be called the Jews, after the Kingdom of Judah).

Of the many stories and events that mark the relationship between God and the Israelites, none is more important than what the biblical authors recount in the second book of the Hebrew Scriptures, the Book of Exodus, which begins with the Israelites enslaved in Egypt. Witnessing this oppression, God selects Moses to lead the Israelites out of slavery and into freedom, into the land that God had promised to Abraham. What follow are some of the most well-known stories of the Bible: Moses' confrontation with the Pharaoh, the parting of the sea, the deliverance of the Ten Commandments, and the forty-year journey of the Israelites through the desert.

The exodus and the journey through the desert remain central to Jewish theology and identity, but they also provide themes that carry into Christianity. In this story, we see a God who cares for his people; a God who calls us to cherish community, live morally, and be kind to strangers. As God tells Moses, "You shall not wrong or oppress a resident alien, for you were aliens in the land of Egypt. You shall not abuse any widow or orphan. If you do abuse them, when they cry out to me, I will surely heed their cry" (Exod 22:21–23).

The rest of the Old Testament chronicles the ups and downs of the Israelites as they struggle to love God and remain faithful to him. In the process, they attempt to absorb and live out the revolutionary idea that the God who called Abraham is not one God among many, but is the only God. The words of the Book of Deuteronomy remain central to the worship of the Jewish people: "Hear, O Israel: The LORD is our God, the LORD alone. You shall love the LORD your God with all your heart, and with all your soul, and with all your might" (6:4–5).

A Personal God

In God's self-disclosure to the Israelites, God revealed himself to be a fundamentally personal God. By the use of the word *personal*, the Catholic Church does not mean that God is a person like you and me. Rather, the Catholic tradition uses the word *personal* analogically—as an analogy to communicate something essential about God. To say that God is a "personal" God means that God revealed himself to have characteristics we normally associate with persons, such as "intelligence, love, compassion, graciousness, fidelity, and especially the *capacity for relationship*."[9] This can be seen in the Book of Jeremiah: "For surely I know the plans I have for you, says the LORD, plans for your welfare and not for harm, to give you a future with hope. Then when you call upon me and come and pray to me, I will hear you" (29:11–12).

Throughout the Old Testament, God shows himself to be deeply interested in human affairs. The Divine Reality we discussed in the previous chapter is not an unconscious or uncaring force. He is a God, rather, who desires to enter into relationship with human beings, and this relationship begins with the Hebrews/

Israelites, starting with the call of Abraham and Sarah. Through his interactions and encounters with the Israelites, God showed us that he is one (there are no other gods), that he is loving and forgiving, and that if humans abide his teachings, we will achieve a holy, flourishing life.

However, the history of God's self-disclosure does not end there. Christians believe in something even more magnificent: God not only inspired the human authors of the Bible; God himself also entered into human history. God came to us "in the flesh" in and through the person of Jesus Christ.

CHAPTER SEVEN

The Person
of Jesus

The resurrection of Jesus Christ is a magnificent event, and for good reason: The celebration of this event, which takes place on Easter Sunday, is considered the most important day of the Christian calendar. The resurrection is the sign, the confirmation, of one of the most fundamental beliefs of Christianity, the belief that God became man.

As we discussed in the previous chapter, in and through God's self-disclosure to the Israelites, God revealed himself to be one who desires relationship, not for any need of his own, but for our sake. Starting with Abraham, expanding to Abraham's family and eventually to the entire Israelite people, God began to teach humanity how to live with one another, how to relate to God, and how to love.

That claim itself is remarkable, but Christians believe God went further. Christians believe that God not only disclosed himself to the Hebrew people, but that he also entered into

71

human history, not symbolically or figuratively, but truly and actually. Christians believe that God embodied himself in and through the person of Jesus Christ.

Two Cautions Concerning Jesus

First, Jesus might be the most analyzed person in human history, and what I say will necessarily be incomplete. Second, in considering the life of Jesus, it's absolutely crucial that you once more take stock of your background theories. It is tempting to approach the subject of Jesus with a range of preconceived notions shaped according to our culture, ideology, or belief systems. It's remarkable how often people assume things about Jesus that are totally unsupported by evidence or that arise from mere opinion or distortions found in the media. The life of Jesus is not a blank canvas on which we paint whatever we want. Jesus came at a specific time and place, within the political and religious context of first-century Palestine.

Historical Background

In 930 BCE, the nation of Israel split into two: the northern kingdom became the Kingdom of Israel and the southern kingdom became the Kingdom of Judah. Then, as now, territory was never secure, and the two kingdoms constantly faced threats. In 722 BCE, Assyria conquered the Kingdom of Israel and exiled much of the Hebrew population. In 604 BCE, Babylonia invaded Judah and eventually destroyed the city of Jerusalem and the Jewish Temple. From approximately 587 BCE to 537 BCE, the Babylonians exiled Judah's inhabitants to Babylonia.

These defeats devastated the Israelites, not just in terms of their living space, but also in terms of their relationship with God. The Babylonians and the Assyrians worshipped many gods and engaged in other practices (for example, child sacrifice)[1] that contradicted the terms of the covenant between God and Israel. From Old Testament writings, we know that many of the captured Israelites began to turn away from their beliefs and adopt some of the objectionable behaviors of their captors.

In the wake of these trials, some Israelites began to speak about someone who would liberate the Jewish people. As God had done long ago in Egypt, he would once again free the Israelites from their captivity and restore the nation of Israel. The prophet Jeremiah proclaimed, "The days are surely coming, says the LORD, when I will raise up for David a righteous Branch, and he shall reign as king and deal wisely, and shall execute justice and righteousness in the land. In his days Judah will be saved and Israel will live in safety." (Jer 23:5–6).

Earlier, in the Book of Deuteronomy, Moses had told the Israelites, "The LORD your God will raise up for you a prophet like me from among your own people; you shall heed such a prophet" (18:15). In the Book of Chronicles, the Lord (through the prophet Nathan) tells King David, "I will raise up your offspring after you, one of your own sons, and I will establish his kingdom. He shall build a house for me, and I will establish his throne forever. I will be a father to him, and he shall be a son to me....I will confirm him in my house and in my kingdom forever, and his throne shall be established forever" (1 Chr 17:11–14).

A few hundred years before the birth of Jesus, the Prophet Isaiah spoke about a "servant" of the Lord:

> He was despised and rejected by others;
>   a man of suffering and acquainted with infirmity;
> and as one from whom others hide their faces
>   he was despised, and we held him of no account.

Surely he has borne our infirmities
and carried our diseases;
yet we accounted him stricken,
struck down by God, and afflicted.
But he was wounded for our transgressions,
crushed for our iniquities;
upon him was the punishment that made us whole,
and by his bruises we are healed.

(Isa 53:3–5)

Isaiah went on to say that this servant "bore the sin of many, / and made intercession for the transgressors" (Isa 53:12).

In addition to Isaiah speaking of a "suffering servant," the prophet Jeremiah announced that God would make a new covenant: "The days are surely coming, says the LORD, when I will make a new covenant with the house of Israel and the house of Judah" (Jer 31:31).

Additional passages in the Hebrew Scriptures convey a similar message. Though there are differences, they converge around the theme of expectation. The authors believed that someone would come who would restore and redeem Israel, even, perhaps, create a new covenant. How this person would go about the saving and redeeming was not entirely clear. Nevertheless, the prophets writing in the Old Testament "held out the hope that God would again intervene in the life of the people, showing the divine loving kindness, destroying the evil oppressing them, and manifesting the salvation that only God could bring."[2]

Jesus the Redeemer

The New Testament tells the story of Jesus Christ, the savior and redeemer. Early Christians identified Jesus Christ as the suffering servant spoken of in Isaiah, the "new Moses" prophesied in Deuteronomy, and "the son of God" whose kingdom would last forever identified in the Book of Chronicles.

In summary, the redeemer and the savior came as expected, but he did not come to save the Israelites only. He was not a political or military savior. He did not arrive to overthrow the Romans or restore the Jewish political kingdom. Jesus came for a much different purpose: to announce that the reign of God was at hand. As Jesus himself said, "My kingdom is not from this world. If my kingdom were from this world, my followers would be fighting to keep me from being handed over to the Jews. But as it is, my kingdom is not from here" (John 18:36). Jesus came to spread the kingdom of God. He came to make God present in our midst. For Christians, Jesus isn't a representative of God; Jesus *is* God. Jesus is the embodiment of God, or "God in the flesh." This is the "incarnation," from the Latin words *in* (in) and *caro* (flesh). The mystery of the incarnation refers to the mystery of God assuming a human form.

Jesus came to convert hearts and minds, to teach and show us how to live as sons and daughters of God. He did so by preaching, by performing miracles, and most of all, by conquering death, a miraculous event known as the resurrection. Indeed, it's perhaps more proper to say that Catholics believe that Jesus had to live, die, and rise from the dead. The resurrection of Jesus was, and remains, the ultimate sign of Jesus' identity as God in the flesh. This was the event that changed history and gave rise to Christianity.

The Source

One of the main sources for the claim that God became a human being and rose from the dead is the second section of the

Bible—the New Testament. The New Testament is comprised of twenty-seven books devoted to Jesus and to the movement that began in the wake of his resurrection, the movement we call "Christianity." Most people are familiar with the first four books, or Gospels, of the New Testament. We attribute these Gospels to the work of four evangelists: Matthew, Mark, Luke, and John. The word *gospel* means "good news." The "good news" these writers proclaimed was the saving mission of Jesus through his life, death, and resurrection.

In addition to the writings of the New Testament (Scripture), the teaching of the Church (Tradition) clarifies the nature and mission of Jesus. The New Testament is not self-interpreting, and over the course of the first few centuries, leaders in the Church communicated precisely who Jesus was and what he meant, as these leaders continue to do today.

One of the most important tasks of the early Church was articulating Jesus' identity. "Jesus Christ" is a combination of a name and a title. The name *Jesus* is the Greek form of the Hebrew name *Joshua*, which means "God saves." *Christ* derives from a Greek word that means "the anointed one," and is a translation of the Hebrew word *messiah*. "Christ," therefore, is not Jesus' last name; it is his title.[3] Referring to Jesus as "the Anointed One" or as "the Messiah" is a way of saying that he was the long-awaited redeemer, or savior, that Old Testament authors, especially the prophets, had spoken about.[4]

In recognizing Jesus as the Christ, we believe that Jesus is not a mere representative of God, nor an exceptionally holy human being whom God appointed for a temporary mission. He is not a political revolutionary. For Christians, the belief is far more important: Jesus Christ is God. In Christ, the ultimate Reality, the Reality who is the source of all existence, the Reality who revealed himself to the Hebrews, has become a human being.

Jesus of History versus the Christ of Faith

Some people question whether Jesus lived. They sometimes assume that early Christians made up the person of Jesus for political or religious reasons, and like some of my students, they sweep Jesus into the category of myth.

However, as noted earlier, we must rely not upon wishful thinking or background theories but on credible reasons. There is no serious dispute that Jesus lived. Christians did not make him up. In fact, N. T. Wright, a well-known biblical scholar, said, "The evidence for Jesus is so massive that, as a historian, I want to say we have got almost as much good evidence for Jesus as for anyone in the ancient world."[5] Luke Timothy Johnson, a professor of New Testament and Christian Origins at Emory University, said, "Even the most critical historian can confidently assert that a Jew named Jesus worked as a teacher and wonder-worker in Palestine during the reign of Tiberius, and continued to have followers after his death."[6] Finally, Bart Ehrman, the non-Christian biblical scholar and historian of early Christianity, said, "The Christians did not invent Jesus....Whether we like it or not, Jesus certainly existed."[7]

The more pressing issue is whether Jesus did what Christians say he did—whether Jesus performed miracles and rose from the dead, thereby revealing and confirming his identity as God in the flesh. To say that Jesus lived is a historical reality; to say that this Jesus is also "the Christ" is a statement of religious faith. For this is really what Christianity turns on. We believe, in the words of Luke Timothy Johnson, that "after his crucifixion and burial Jesus entered into the powerful life of God, and shares that life...with those who can receive it."[8] We believe, in other words, in the resurrection. What is the resurrection? The Christian claim of Jesus' resurrection:

> ...is not that he picked up his old manner of life, but rather that after his death he entered into an entirely new form of existence, one in which he shared the power of God and in which he could share that power with others. The resurrection experience, then, is not simply something that happened to Jesus but is equally something that happened to Jesus' followers. The sharing in Jesus' new life through the power of the Holy Spirit is an essential dimension of the resurrection. This power of new life, furthermore, is understood by Christians to be the basis for claiming that they are part of a new creation, and a new form of humanity shaped according to the image of the resurrected One.[9]

The amount of literature on the resurrection is overwhelming, and it's impossible to cover this question fully. But this doesn't mean we are left in complete mystery. As we noted earlier, we live within a horizon of uncertainty, but this doesn't mean we proceed blindly. We balance our uncertainty with credible reasons to believe. On what grounds, for what reasons, might we believe in this most important of claims that Jesus is the resurrected Son of God?

Credible Reasons for the Resurrection

In the first century and continuing forward, many Jews who became followers of Christ radically changed their understanding of the concept of "resurrection." N. T. Wright says that, in the first century, there were "several modifications in the classic Jewish belief about resurrection."[10] In fact, Wright identifies seven such modifications. For example, in early Christianity, the concept of resurrection "moved from being one doctrine among many others—important, but not that important—which is where it is in Judaism, to become the center of everything. Take it away from Paul, say, or 1 Peter, Revelation, or the great second-century fathers, and you will destroy their whole framework."[11] These drastic modifications are evidence of something big: "We have to conclude that something must have happened to bring 'resurrection' in from the periphery to the center, to the focal point."[12]

Wright adds that early Christians "are remarkably unanimous in their view not only of resurrection as their belief, but of how resurrection plays out and how it works."[13] The "wide extent and unanimity of early Christian belief in resurrection force us to say that something definite *happened*, way back early on, that has shaped and colored the whole early Christian movement."[14]

Were the resurrection accounts made up? Wright addresses this issue as well. Wright says that the evidence makes that explanation unlikely. He argues, for example, that if you were a first-century Jew inventing a story about Jesus' resurrection, your "natural biblical source" would be the Book of Daniel, from the Old Testament. The Book of Daniel says that those who have resurrected will shine like stars. But the resurrection accounts in the New Testament, notes Wright, are not consistent with the Book of Daniel. The Gospels do not portray Jesus shining like a star. In sum, "the portrait of Jesus in the resurrection narratives is very, very odd. It's not what you would expect. There is no portrait like that in the Jewish narratives of the time."[15]

Naturally, questions arise: Why the change? Why did radically new beliefs about the resurrection suddenly pop up? According to Wright, the answer is clear: "Something extraordinary has happened that's left its footprints in the narratives. People would not have made these things up off the tops of their heads. Anyone writing fictitious accounts of Easter would have made Jesus more clearly recognizable."[16]

Finally, Wright concludes that "in order to explain the rise of early Christianity...we have to say that the very early church really did believe that Jesus had been bodily raised from the dead. We have no evidence of any very early Christians who believed anything else."[17]

Luke Timothy Johnson agrees, claiming "that some sort of powerful, transformative experience is required to generate the sort of movement earliest Christianity was, and to necessitate the sort of literature the New Testament is."[18]

Note that N. T. Wright, Luke Timothy Johnson, and many others are *not* arguing that we have incontrovertible evidence that Jesus rose from the dead. That's impossible.[19] Their point is that certain historical developments and certain changes in religious belief are best explained by proposing that Jesus in fact rose from the dead.

In other words, the developments in first-century Palestine raise certain questions: Why did so many Jews suddenly adopt such radical beliefs about the meaning of resurrection? Why did non-Jews adopt beliefs about resurrection that, in the context of the pagan world, were seen as ridiculous? And why did so many people change their entire lives, even giving up their lives, for this new belief—the belief that Jesus was the long-awaited Messiah? For N. T. Wright, Luke Timothy Johnson, and others, the best explanation is that Jesus rose from the dead.

Discussions about the resurrection of Jesus tend to raise many questions and objections. For two thousand years, people have been proposing alternative theories for the empty tomb. For example: Jesus' followers stole his body; Jesus didn't really die on the cross; the resurrection narratives were the product of mass delusion; Jesus' followers made up the story of Jesus' resurrection.

Regardless of the particular theory, many good books address these claims and explain why they are untrue or ridiculous.

There are many additional reasons to believe that Jesus rose from the dead, and to be sure, none are conclusive. There is no single piece of evidence that demonstrates, once and for all, that Jesus conquered death. Ultimately, we have to make a leap of faith. However, believers don't make this leap blindly, merely because we want it to be true. We can come to believe in Jesus' resurrection, or at least become open to the possibility of Jesus' resurrection, because there are credible reasons for doing so.

Jesus Has Risen. Now What?

Though the resurrection of Jesus is one of the foundations of Christian belief, we do not become practicing Christians merely because we acknowledge the resurrection or believe that it occurred. Christians don't think about Jesus like we think about Abraham Lincoln or the Civil War, as an event in the past from which we draw lessons but which doesn't have any ongoing spiritual impact. Christians seek to live like Jesus, to follow his teachings, and to be in relationship with him. Christians believe in the importance of the Church and in the community of believers Jesus has inspired and drawn together. Christians believe that the example of Christ continues to transform lives in the here and now. In practical terms, what does this mean?

CHAPTER EIGHT

The Calling

As Greg continued to lie in a coma, and as friends and family began to absorb the seriousness of his injuries, my colleagues and I began to contemplate how we might bring hope to our tearful students and friends. As members of a Catholic school community, we turned to the resources and wisdom of our Christian faith and decided to hold a prayer service.

We chose a location a few hundred yards from Greg's intensive care room, a small portico connected to a lovely facility called the Hansen House. We centered the service on New Testament readings that illuminated three aspects of Jesus: Jesus as healer, as comforter, and as friend. We asked Jesus to heal Greg, to comfort us in our sorrow, and to be with us as a companion. We appealed to Jesus, trusting that he wanted to be involved in our lives and in the messiness of our grief and misfortune.

Reaching this point along the faith journey takes time. It can be difficult to see Jesus as a friend or as someone who wants to be in relationship with us. How, then, do we better understand who Jesus is and what he asks of us?

Seeking Jesus

Understanding the rich and layered life of Jesus can be overwhelming. For example, consider these facts: Jesus, a Jew, was born in Palestine, which at the time was under the control of the Roman Empire. The official language of the Empire was Latin, but the common language of the Empire was Greek. Many Jews also knew Hebrew (the language of their Sacred Scriptures), but people also spoke other dialects, such as Aramaic, the native language of Jesus.

Gaining a complete picture of Jesus and the New Testament requires extensive knowledge of language, history, archaeology, and the various religious groups and political dynamics of the first century. Moreover, the New Testament itself doesn't necessarily provide a way to tie all these aspects together. Christ heals the sick, he demonstrates mastery over the elements, he shocks religious authorities, he calls people to follow him, and he tells short stories with life and spiritual lessons—the narratives within narratives we call "parables," like the parable of the prodigal son or the parable of the Good Samaritan, two of the most well-known of these stories. He speaks about the "Spirit" and the "Father," and on many occasions, he references, sometimes obscurely, verses from the Hebrew Scriptures (the Old Testament).

Jesus is a controversial figure who provokes and mystifies. At one point, he says, "Do not be afraid, little flock, for it is your Father's good pleasure to give you the kingdom" (Luke 12:32), and then a short time later adds, "I came to bring fire to the earth, and how I wish it were already kindled!" (12:49). With similar boldness, he declares, "I am the way, and the truth, and the life. No one comes to the Father except through me" (John 14:6).

Faced with this variety, it can be difficult to know where to begin. Therefore, in the chapters that follow, we will focus on two themes that provide interpretive keys for understanding the stories, parables, and episodes that make up Jesus' public activity: the call of Christ and the invitation to *metanoia*.

The Call of Christ

One of the most important aspects of the relationship between Jesus and his creation is "the call." The Gospel of Mark reports,

> As Jesus passed along the Sea of Galilee, he saw Simon and his brother Andrew casting a net into the sea—for they were fishermen. And Jesus said to them, "Follow me and I will make you fish for people." And immediately they left their nets and followed him. As he went a little farther, he saw James son of Zebedee and his brother John, who were in their boat mending the nets. Immediately he called them; and they left their father Zebedee in the boat with the hired men, and followed him. (1:16–20)

This pattern continues throughout Jesus' ministry. One of the most well-known of these calls, as noted in chapter 2, is the call of the person whom many refer to as the "rich young man." The Gospel of Matthew describes it like this:

> Then someone came to him and said, "Teacher, what good deed must I do to have eternal life?" And he said to him, "Why do you ask me about what is good? There is only one who is good. If you wish to enter into life,

keep the commandments." He said to him, "Which ones?" And Jesus said, "You shall not murder; You shall not commit adultery; You shall not steal; You shall not bear false witness; Honor your father and mother; also, You shall love your neighbor as yourself." The young man said to him, "I have kept all these; what do I still lack?" Jesus said to him, "If you wish to be perfect, go, sell your possessions, and give the money to the poor, and you will have treasure in heaven; then come, follow me." (19:16–21)

The above passages demonstrate a pattern that recurs frequently in the Gospels: Jesus invites people to join him, to be with him, and to see his way of life.

In calling people to follow him, Jesus is making a statement not only about what he knows but about who he is and what he does. If he only wanted us to accumulate knowledge, he could do that from afar, through sermons or books. But this isn't what Jesus desires. Jesus desires people to witness his actions, meet the people he encounters, and imitate his lifestyle. He, himself, is what he needs to convey. As Joseph Ratzinger (later Pope Benedict XVI) stated, "The person of Jesus is his teaching, and his teaching is he himself. Christian faith, that is, faith in Jesus as the Christ, is therefore truly 'personal faith.'"[1]

Furthermore, in calling people to follow him, Jesus is repeating something we see often in the Old Testament. In fact, the Jesus who calls people in the New Testament is the same God who calls people in the Old. The Old Testament contains numerous examples of God reaching out to people to invite them to a new life, a new condition, or a new way of thinking. He calls Abraham, for example, to move to a new land, bear children, and enter into a covenant with God. He calls Moses to free the Hebrews from the Egyptians. He calls David to be king. He calls prophets to speak on his behalf.

God makes a similar invitation to us. In ways unique to our lives and circumstances, God calls us to join him to work for the Kingdom of God.

Features of the Call

The recurrence of "the call" in the Bible, especially in the New Testament, teaches us lessons about the divine–human relationship.

God takes the initiative. It is the Creator who opens the mind and heart of the creature. In the words of Pope Francis, "God does not wait for us to go to him. But it is he who moves toward us, without calculation, without quantification. That is what God is like. He always takes the first step; he comes toward us."[2]

Reflecting on this "divine first step" deepens our understanding of what it means to believe. Earlier, we noted that all acts of faith are acts of entrustment. We entrust ourselves to realities, conditions, people, and hoped-for futures. The act of religious faith also involves entrustment, but God enables us to give it. Fr. Robert Barron captures it well:

> "To believe," as Jesus uses the term, signals, not so much a way of knowing as a way of *being known*. To have faith is to allow oneself to be overwhelmed by the power of God, to permit the divine energy to reign at all levels of one's being. As such, it is not primarily a matter of understanding and assenting to propositions as it is surrendering to the God who wants to become incarnate in us.[3]

Here Barron implies that faith in God is ultimately about letting God take root in—become incarnate in—our own hearts and souls. But this receptivity is not something we humans create, construct, or bring about. It is not like cracking a code, solving a math problem, or earning a promotion. Although this is perhaps a strange analogy, it is not unlike surfing. Observing surfers, they wax their boards, put on wetsuits, and paddle out into the ocean. Once there, they surrender to the natural movements of the water. They don't force a wave to carry them to the shore. They haven't designed the scientific laws that create the waves in the first place. They put themselves in a position to catch the wave and wait. They are patient, attentive, and mindful. Eventually, the right wave arrives and delivers them to the shore.

Likewise, we must surrender ourselves to God. We surrender to the wave of the Divine Reality, which is constantly moving around us, but which is sometimes too subtle for us to notice. What is that wave? Perhaps it's a person you meet, a book you come across, or a thought that you've never had before. Maybe it's a traumatic event or a joyful one. Regardless of the cause, there are times in life when something totally out of the ordinary occurs and it begins to lead us into a different kind of existence that seems tinged with a presence beyond this world.

The surfing analogy points us toward another important idea: faith as a gift. It's something we receive, not something we impose. It's similar to falling in love: We cannot force ourselves to fall in love, and we cannot force someone else to love us. We can, however, take actions that make falling in love and attracting the love of another more likely. If a man abuses his health, mismanages his finances, and refuses to socialize, his chances of finding a spouse will be lower than if he exercises regularly, keeps a clean home, holds a good job, and regularly dates. However, no matter what we might do to attract a spouse, falling in love is still a gift. It is something gratuitous. It is something we don't summon at will.

The same holds for faith in God. We can do many things to prepare for and nurture the gift of faith. As noted in prior chapters, we can clear our minds of preconceived notions, we can survey our context and understand the ways it has shaped our judgments about prayer and the spiritual life, and we can reflect upon the created world and centuries of human experience to examine the evidence of a Divine Reality. However, God must bridge the gap. God must give us the ability to believe.

What Guides Our Lives?

The call of Christ also presents decisive questions for our lives: To whom do we belong? For what purpose do we live?

Prior to the call, we might be living honorable lives, but our decisions might reflect mostly worldly goals. But human beings, as St. Thomas Aquinas reminds us, are made for a supernatural end. We are made for more than this world, for eternal life with God. This becomes evident in Jesus' dialogue with the rich young man. According to the story, this man has done well. He seems to be not only living morally but also excelling financially.

As the Gospel reports, after hearing Jesus' response—to sell his possessions and follow him—"he went away grieving, for he had many possessions" (Matt 19:22). Jesus had essentially asked this man to reverse course, to recalibrate his criteria for happiness and success. The Gospel says nothing more about the rich young man, but the encounter teaches us something crucial about turning our lives over to Jesus. When Christ summons and we say yes, we give him the keys to our future. His desires become the guiding lights for our lives.

Now, facing such a decision can unsettle and uproot. For those men and women in the New Testament who heard such a call, it possibly confused and irritated them, leaving them to wonder: What is this person calling us to? What does he seek from us?

Jesus doesn't address details. When Christ asks people to join him, he doesn't talk about healthcare and salary. The question

"What's in it for me?" is not the response Jesus is looking for. The kingdom of the world operates that way but not the Kingdom of God. We are to entrust ourselves to God because he is God, the One through whom our existence has meaning.

While this may seem daunting, remember that Jesus is the divine physician. He calls us to restore us. Jesus says, "Peace I leave with you; my peace I give to you. I do not give to you as the world gives. Do not let your hearts be troubled, and do not let them be afraid" (John 14:27). Accepting Christ in our lives can sometimes cause inner turmoil as we strive to die to self and live like him. However, where worldly affairs can bring us trouble and insecurity, Christ brings wholeness and serenity. He is the source of our lives. If someone asks, "Why should I give my faith to Christ?" the response is "Because that is where your happiness will be." Christ is the one who knows how we work. When Jesus calls us, he is doing so not for him but for us. His call is an act of continuing creation by the One who is, at his core, a creator.

Sensing God's Call?

Though God can speak to us directly or in a way that's unmistakable, many people tend to experience God's call as they prayerfully reflect upon the events and experiences in their lives. For example, St. Ignatius of Loyola, the founder of a Catholic religious order known as the Society of Jesus, believed that we could sense God's will in feelings of consolation and desolation, in the feelings evoked by certain thoughts or contemplations. For St. Ignatius, peace and optimism were signs that God was at work in those thoughts. As a good friend of mine says, "God speaks to us within the movements of our hearts."

Some people detect God's call in spectacular ways, in a form or fashion that is unmistakable; for others, it's subtler.

One well-known story is that of Jesuit priest and author Fr. James Martin, SJ.

In his memoir, *In Good Company*, Martin recalls that in his mid-twenties, he was advancing up the corporate ladder at General Electric, destined for a lucrative career as a GE executive. Despite this success, he grew unhappy. He wrote,

> I was making a great salary, had a good deal of independence and control at work, and was moving up in the company. But those things in themselves didn't bring me much satisfaction. Simply put, I couldn't figure out the point of what I was doing with my life. Something basic was missing. I enjoyed my coworkers and some of the work in human resources, but what was the point of the work itself? Is this life?[4]

As he remained stuck in those questions, Martin described coming home at night after a terrible day. He had dealt with an anxious employee who wanted to quit. He'd have to work on the weekend. He was tired and feeling sick. Rather than make dinner, he decided to watch TV.

What Martin saw next changed his life. He came across a PBS special on Thomas Merton, one of the most famous Catholics of the twentieth century. The special so intrigued Martin that he went out and bought *The Steven Storey Mountain*, Merton's spiritual autobiography, which tells of Merton's journey from being an atheist to becoming a Catholic, and from his life as a writer in New York City to becoming a Catholic monk in Kentucky.

The book electrified Martin. Reading about Merton entering the monastery, Martin said, "Wow. I realized with some force that this was what I could do....It sounded great—so peaceful, so romantic. I couldn't get his story out of my mind, and read the book three times." Soon afterward, Martin began reading other iconic works, including C. S. Lewis's account of his conversion, *Surprised by Joy*.

Merton's story inspired Martin to learn more about the priestly life. He investigated religious orders and, eventually, he couldn't stop thinking about becoming a priest. Within a couple years, Martin joined the Jesuits. He had heard and answered the call.

What If I Don't Believe in God or Sense His Call?

In the above example, Martin believed that God was moving his heart through certain experiences and was willing to believe that God was acting in the ordinary. But what if you're not ready to do that? What if you're struggling to believe in God's existence? What if you're not sure whether God is reaching out to you?

First, it's important to acknowledge these questions and spend time with them. Don't ignore them, as they might lead you to important insights about your assumptions and presuppositions concerning your faith. Ask yourself what it is precisely that you find hard to believe or accept. Do you doubt God's existence? Do you struggle to believe that he could come to meet humans in the person of Jesus? Regardless of your concerns, don't try to rush past them. You may benefit from additional reading and reflection. If you're not ready to think about Jesus, that is OK. Your timeline is your own.

Second, ask yourself whether, even in the midst of your doubt, you can remain open to the possibility of God's existence and God's willingness to reach out to you. Can you say, "Even though I'm confused and unsure about God and Jesus, I will still leave open the possibility that he might exist and might communicate with me"? Part of the nature of faith is that we don't have to be 100 percent certain of something to be open to its presence in our lives. All acts of entrustment involve risk that we might be wrong. What possibilities open up to you, however, if you're willing to take that risk?

Third, if you are open to God's involvement in your life, be attentive to the ways he might be communicating with you. In her book *Chasing Mystery*, Carey Walsh wrote, "Divine presence is inviting rather than coercive."[5] This is different from the world's way of proceeding. The world shoves images and advertisements right in our line of sight, begging us to take a course of action. The world coerces so that we might consume. But God, notes Walsh, often works differently. He might be hiding in plain sight, simply waiting for us to notice. How is he doing so? Maybe someone you recently met is starting to transform your perception about yourself and life, and in good ways. Maybe you've sensed a desire to start a new hobby or a new career, and you notice feelings of joy and peace when you contemplate doing so. Maybe you have felt inspired to call someone you haven't spoken to in a long time and reconnect. It could be a number of things, but if we observe something slightly out of the ordinary, something drawing us into a new space of awareness, thoughtfulness, or inspiration, it might be God tapping us on the shoulder.

The Journey

Although biblical figures often undertake a literal journey in response to God's call, we should not conceive of the call strictly in those terms. The physical journeys biblical figures undertake highlight the more significant voyages they embark upon in their hearts. The dropping of the fishing nets and the relinquishing of wealth—the examples from Mark and Matthew we cited above—

serve as visible signs of inner decisions. Often, a physical or geo-graphic relocation helps reinforce that decision, but it's not essential.

The specific nature of God's call depends upon a person's unique spiritual condition. Not all of us will be called like the apos-tles or the rich young man. Some might be called to relinquish money, while others might be called to use their money more char-itably; others might be called to a new career. Some might be called out of the single life and into marriage; while others might be called to the priesthood or religious life. It might involve a combi-nation of roles or tasks. Everyone has a unique vocation.[6]

The call of God might involve more than a life-changing vocation. Some might be called to change an attitude. In the parable of the prodigal son, for example, the father at the center of the narrative appears to be well off, but the parable doesn't condemn this abundance. Rather, the parable critiques the atti-tude of the older brother. The older brother is jealous and envi-ous of his younger sibling, feelings that derive from a businesslike, transactional view of human relationships. In this case, the older brother isn't called to relinquish material items, but rather, to relinquish his stingy and ungrateful attitude.

It's not necessarily the case that the call will include a dra-matic and life-altering moment, as in the manner in which Christ calls the apostles. But what, after all, is a life-altering moment? For some people, a move across the country and a change in careers is easier than picking up the phone and saying "I'm sorry" to a family member. Perhaps you meet someone in a parking lot, maybe a homeless person who needs your help. You may be called to drop the "net" of your agenda and respond. Perhaps a friend needs you to visit him or her in the hospital. Perhaps a coworker needs your mercy.

These acts, too, are part of the call of Christ. They are no less important than changing a career or entering the religious life.

No matter what God calls us to do, he does so to make us whole, not to make us miserable. God calls us away from the actions, habits, and behaviors that limit our freedom. In the words of Jesus himself, "I came that they may have life, and have it abundantly" (John 10:10).

When we recognize that call, how will we respond?

CHAPTER NINE

Conversion

When Jesus enters our lives and summons us to a new path, he is not asking for a one-time commitment. This is not a temporary mission.

A key to understanding what's at stake can be found in the opening chapter of the Gospel of Mark. Before he begins his ministry, Jesus announces, "The kingdom of God has come near; repent, and believe in the good news" (1:15).

The word *repent* comes from the Greek word *metanoia*, which combines two words: *meta*, meaning "beyond," and *nous*, meaning "mind." Commenting upon this term and its Greek roots, Fr. Robert Barron has observed that *metanoia* involves going beyond one's mind, a transcending of one's normal way of thinking.¹ Some scholars frame *metanoia* in terms of a complete change of mind and heart, a sort of remodeling of one's inner life. By using this word, therefore, Jesus is telling his followers, *The Kingdom of God is at hand, and I am calling you to change your minds and hearts to embrace, embody, and reflect the reality of God's presence and love.*

Another word we could use to describe this transformation of heart and mind is *conversion*, which derives from the Latin word meaning "to turn around." When one converts, one changes direction. Books, movies, and articles are filled with "conversion stories," and *convert* is usually applied to those who undergo a significant change in religious belief or worldview.

Whether we characterize these changes as conversion, *metanoia*, or transformation, the message is clear: Christ calls us to transform our way of thinking and our way of living to embrace the kingdom of God. St. Paul tells us, "Do not be conformed to this world, but be transformed by the renewing of your minds" (Rom 12:2). Once we encounter Christ, we can't keep doing things or living the same way. The experience of *metanoia* involves acknowledging our sins, our shortcomings, and all the ways we have obscured or missed the Divine Reality.

While this concept might seem difficult to grasp and the Greek language somewhat off-putting, the experience of *metanoia* is quite common. Transformations of mind and heart happen frequently, but they aren't always connected with what we'd call a "religious experience."

Consider what happens when two people fall in love. When people fall in love, they tend to experience something like a *metanoia*. They adopt new interests, smile more, and approach the day with a freshness that makes the commonplace extraordinary. For example, when I met my wife, I began to explore subjects—like art and music—that I had long neglected. Because of her inspiration and because I wanted to share in what she loved and cared for, I began to dance. I wanted to participate in what makes her so magnificent. After we started dating, a road that I had driven on hundreds of times suddenly became the landscape of something sacred. Why? It was the road I had to take to get to her house. In short, I had a transformation of mind and heart.

Though a core part of me stayed the same, I became, in many ways, a new man. I had a *metanoia*.

Another experience of *metanoia* occurred after graduating from Notre Dame Law School. During my early twenties, I was searching for an arrangement of professional and material success that would permit me a relatively untroubled happiness. During my first year in practice, frustration mounted. All the things I had assumed would make me happy were not. And the more I tried to enjoy them, the more stifled I felt. Eventually, I began to ruminate on my life and my Catholic education, pining to connect with more soul-nourishing work. I wanted to be alert and alive, excited to go to work. I didn't want to think, as Fr. Martin did at General Electric, "Is this it?"

As I examined my choices and priorities, suddenly a new desire began to emerge: I didn't want to be successful only on the terms of this world. I wanted to be successful on the terms of the gospel. I began to conceive of myself as a "disciple," as one who follows Jesus. What did the call to follow Jesus mean for me? Was it enough to be a virtuous person or was something more demanded?

Over the course of the year, I began thinking that God might be inviting me back to the arena from which I had just come: Catholic education. I decided to leave my law practice to teach theology at a new Catholic high school in Palm Desert, California.

It was liberating but also confusing. I had studied thousands of hours and taken out six figures in loans. Now I was teaching theology at a Catholic school. It didn't make sense.

Nevertheless, despite my confusion, I was happy and fulfilled. After months of discernment, I began to imagine a new version of success. This version, I knew, might not include prestige or a high salary, but those concerns drifted out of focus. I began to see myself as successful only to the extent that I remained open to God's call. I didn't know if I was going to be a teacher forever.

I didn't know if I was going to return to the practice of law. I did know, however, that I was right where I needed to be. Christ promises a "peace not of this world," and this is what I felt.

Faith and *Metanoia*

When Christ announces that the kingdom of God is at hand, he wants us to fall in love with the kingdom like we fall in love with a spouse. He wants us to see the world through new eyes— through *his* eyes. These are eyes of love, compassion, and forgiveness. They are eyes of faith and radical freedom. They are the eyes of one who cherishes the people the world often ignores: the poor, the sick, the sinners, and the suffering.

The inspiration for this transformed vision can catch us off guard. At the high school where I teach, we send students on "immersion trips" to places or regions where they can be in solidarity with those who are oppressed or impoverished. Although some students look forward to these trips, others are often nervous and scared. Many of them grow up in comfortable homes, in environments of political and financial security.

After one such summer immersion trip to El Salvador, a student entering her senior year came back to the United States unsettled by what she had seen. Haunted by the poverty and oppression, she returned completely rethinking her life, her goals, and her obligation to those who lacked basic necessities. Until that trip, she had been a competitive volleyball player and hoped to obtain an athletic scholarship. But after her time in El Salvador, she decided to focus not on athletics but on her role in assisting the poor and mending the political and economic harms that keep people oppressed.

Volleyball, at that point, seemed trivial compared to what her conscience now asked of her. So she stopped playing and decided to attend a college or university that focused on service learning. *PeRceive*

This student began to see the world differently. She came back motivated and energized. She was now on a mission. She had felt a call and was ready to respond. She had undergone an encounter that left her reconsidering what she valued. In a word, she had experienced exactly what Christ asks of us: a complete change of mind and heart, a *metanoia*.

The experience of *metanoia* is abundant throughout the Bible and Christian history. Almost without exception, every time people open themselves to the divine will, they alter their priorities, their self-conceptions, and their desires. Many Catholic saints have experienced this radical shift in thinking and in self-conception. One of my favorite stories of *metanoia* is that of St. Ignatius of Loyola.

Ignatius was born in 1491 in the Basque province of Spain. From an early age, he was groomed to be a soldier in service of the Spanish crown. He was a proud man and throughout most of his young life, he seemed to care little for spiritual matters. Local authorities disciplined him for fighting, and by his own admission, Ignatius was a womanizer. In his autobiography, told in the third person, he said that prior to his conversion "he was a man given up to the vanities of the world, and his chief delight used to be in the exercise of arms, with a great and vain desire to gain honour."[2]

These vain desires would end in dramatic fashion. In 1521, the Spanish and French clashed at the Battle of Pamplona, and during the melee, a cannonball shattered Ignatius's right leg and badly wounded the left. Sent to months of recovery in his family's home where he was unable to do anything but rest, Ignatius turned to the only diversions available: books on the lives of the saints and the life of Christ.

His reading and contemplation transformed him. As he dwelled on his life and decisions, and as he imagined the person he wanted to become, he concluded that God was calling him to a different path. He decided to relinquish the conventional career of a soldier and courtier to set upon, in his words, "all the acts of self-denial that a generous spirit, fired with God, generally wants to do."[3]

Desiring to live like Christ and serve the Catholic Church, he eventually returned to school, became a priest, and then, with a group of friends, founded the Jesuits. Rather than seeking the honor of the world, Ignatius spent the rest of his life seeking the glory of God.

Today, the Jesuits are the largest religious order in the world and oversee hundreds of schools and ministries across every continent. It began with an unforeseen cannonball and with Ignatius's *metanoia*.

The Journey Forward

Being open to the nature and scope of what Christ expects of us provides much to reflect upon. It's a long journey. However, the concept of *metanoia* should never stray far from your mind, for it is fundamental in understanding why Christ calls us and what we can expect when that happens. Jesus is not looking for mere compliance with teachings; he is inviting us to a new way of understanding reality.

Like all things in the spiritual life, each person will experience *metanoia* in a way most suitable for him or her. The change or transformation might occur suddenly or unexpectedly in one bold moment, or through a series of little moments over many years. Not everyone requires a cannonball to the leg. Sometimes it's not about changing one's lifestyle or career, but about changing one's attitude or approach to a lifestyle or career. It's not really about whether we marry or where we work but about whether we integrate the habits of mind and heart that Jesus asks of us.

Metanoia can bring difficult times. Change, even good change, can be hard. When people move to a new house or a new city, feelings of happiness can be mixed with uncertainty and sometimes fear. The same can happen when Christ calls us into relationship. Jobs, friendships, and other fixed notions might have to be reevaluated as part of one's spiritual reconfiguring. Christ may invite us into a new set of moral demands, which we may resist at first. Sometimes, as we pray for guidance, we don't receive an obvious message from God, and it takes tremendous patience to persevere. However, remember that Christ does not invite us into this transformation to make us unhappy, but rather to bring us joy.

CHAPTER TEN

A Relationship

In discussions about religion with my students, I have learned that many of them regard Catholicism as a religion that stifles their freedom; as an unnecessarily complex set of prohibitions and doctrines rather than a means by which we access truth, freedom, and goodness.

This impression is not uncommon. When people first start to learn or hear about Catholicism, many assume the practice of the faith centers on rules. Even lifelong Catholics, with a mix of frustration and sorrow, can develop this impression. Some of my Catholic relatives, now over fifty, look back on their early lives—when they were still practicing Catholicism or still willing to give it a chance—and think of Catholicism mostly in terms of regulations and the priests and sisters who enforced them. They speak of a Church too preoccupied with what appeared, to them, to be minute obligations and the fine points of morality. Catholicism, for them, was about making sure they attended Mass, confessed the right number and kind of sins, knew when to eat or not eat meat, and complied with an exacting ethical code. For various reasons, they struggled to see those practices within a larger horizon of meaning and fulfillment. In short, Catholicism is a faith that, in their eyes, lacked a bigger picture or a deeper truth.

This attitude is unfortunate, because Catholicism does not proclaim a system of rules; it proclaims an experience of love. It proclaims that our Creator has entered human history to transform our lives and lead us to wholeness. This is the point of God's call and our response. While this involves acts and behaviors we might call "obligations," these obligations serve and underscore this point: Christianity is fundamentally about a relationship with the living God, specifically Jesus Christ. In the Gospels, Jesus is constantly calling people to be with him—to follow him, to pray with him, and to eat with him. This same personal invitation extends to us today. In the words of Pope Benedict XVI, "Being Christian is not the result of an ethical choice or a lofty idea, but the encounter with an event, a person, which gives life a new horizon and a decisive direction."[1]

In other words, the choice to follow Jesus is not primarily a decision for a rule, a law, or a standard. It is not like becoming an American, which asks people to assent to certain constitutional propositions. In responding to Christ, we are not joining a political party; we are not expressing our advocacy for a list of positions on contested issues. Rather, the choice for Christianity is the decision to align one's life with the God who became one of us.

This doesn't mean that rules or rituals should not be, or cannot be, part of this relationship. Once again, the marital relationship provides a helpful analogy.

If asked to identify the essence of the love between a husband and wife, we would not reduce this essence to compliance with rules and regulations. We would say that marriage connects to something much deeper, for example, the mutual commitment to love and serve one another, the bringing forth of new life, the sharing of emotional and physical joy, and the desire to reflect God's love.

However, beneath those noble principles, we find that their fulfillment depends on a commitment to what we might call duties, obligations, and rituals. The proper honoring of my wife and the proper honoring of my marriage depends on my decision to live morally and to perform actions that make my love concrete. We may love each other, but if we never express that love, if we rarely spend time with each other, if we don't eat dinner together, if we never clean the house or take care of one another, how can we live up to the high ideals we have set for ourselves? In what sense are we honoring our marriage if we don't engage in certain rituals to remind us of the unique nature of our commitment?

Admittedly, one could easily speak of marriage exclusively in light of those rules and obligations. The cynic could reduce marriage to taking out the trash, to eating dinner at least once a week, to bestowing a certain number of compliments, or saying I love you a certain number of times—in other words, someone could easily portray the spousal relationship in language that erases the broader purpose and beauty of that union.

In marriages that break down, frustrated spouses speak in terms of obligations or sacrifices that don't connect to a deeper meaning or purpose. Communication takes the form of retaliation, not forgiveness: *He never helps with the kids; she never lets me see my friends; he works too much; she works too little; he doesn't cook enough; she doesn't cook enough,* and so on. The disappointment sounds like the feelings of those who are disaffected with organized religion, and especially Catholicism. The relationship becomes transactional, not transcendent. It's a faith that has lost its connection with the loving relationship at the heart of the whole project.

Rules and Religious Faith

As in a spousal relationship, Christians should not try to abolish rituals and obligations from their faith, but rather to situate them in their proper context—that is, to see them as supporting and nourishing the relationship between God and us.

For example, consider the sacrament of reconciliation, or what many older Catholics call "confession." In this sacrament, Catholics come to a priest to acknowledge their sins and all the ways they have fallen short in their relationships with God. Through the priest's ministry, God grants them forgiveness. Catholics don't do this to feel awful about past behaviors; rather, we participate in the sacrament of reconciliation to sharpen our consciences and to feel whole again. It's a chance to relieve guilt, not increase it. The sacrament of reconciliation is designed to liberate us from psychological and spiritual burdens, to restore and renew, and to prepare us for the spiritual journey ahead.

The Church invites Catholics to participate in this sacrament to improve their spiritual health, the religious equivalent of going to the doctor. Though some question why the ministry of a priest is necessary and wonder why we cannot just say we're sorry in private, the sacrament of reconciliation honors the natural human need to unburden ourselves to another human being. There is something deeply cleansing and therapeutic in sharing our guilt and sorrow with another; in being totally honest. The sacrament of reconciliation takes this natural human need and provides an opportunity to strengthen one's friendship with Jesus.

Sometimes the Church's teachings and practices are not always welcomed. There are days, for example, when I've gone to Mass more out of compulsion than desire, days when I'm not "feeling" the grace of God or the value of Catholic rituals. There are times when prayer seems to collapse along with a connection with Jesus. In other words, there don't seem to be any spiritual benefits.

However, the same feelings of futility occur in maintaining physical health. There are times that we know we should go to the doctor, but resist. There are times when we have engaged in a course of treatment or in an exercise plan that yields no obvious results. This is when the thought of going to the gym has no appeal, and yet, with patience, we know that exercising will improve our health. On the contrary, if we neglect the right foods and don't exercise, our health will deteriorate and our vital systems will start to shut down.

Similarly, in the life of faith, we are called to give the same trust. During stretches where we don't feel the fruits of our commitment, we are called to commit nonetheless. We are called to believe in spite of appearances.

Nourishing the Relationship

There are various ways we can nourish our relationship with God. Here are four suggestions:

1. prayer
2. reading Scripture
3. accompanying the marginalized
4. participating in the sacraments

PRAYER

To strengthen our relationship with God, we have to communicate with him, and we do that through prayer. Prayer is fundamentally communication with God. We communicate with God about our joys, fears, longings, frustrations, and desires, and we let God communicate with us. In prayer, we become intentionally aware of God's presence in our lives. When we pray, we consciously call to mind our dependence upon the Creator.

The men and women of the Bible provide a model of how to pray. They often address God directly, with a stunning boldness and honesty. For example, the psalmist says, "O LORD, why do you cast me off? / Why do you hide your face from me? / Wretched and close to death from my youth up, / I suffer your terrors; I am desperate" (Ps 88:14–15). Prayer also gives us the opportunity to tell God when we're full of joyful gratitude. Again, the psalmist writes, "Let the nations be glad and sing for joy, / for you judge the peoples with equity / and guide the nations upon earth. Let the peoples praise you, O God; / let all the peoples praise you" (Ps 67:4–5).

There are many forms or methods of prayer. In petitionary prayer, we make a specific request to God. In contemplative prayer, we sit quietly in God's presence, meditating, perhaps upon a word or phrase that keeps us centered and calm. In centering prayer, we let the Divine Life penetrate to the core of our being. It's a chance to let God speak to us, uninterrupted.

There are other methods of prayer, ranging from the formal to the informal and from the elaborate to the simple. Regardless of how we pray, it's important to make ourselves available to God. Even when we feel alone or abandoned by God, it is better that we communicate that sadness in prayer rather than shut down.

READING SCRIPTURE

Reading scripture, the Word of God, can also nourish our bond with God. After all, this is part of the mystery of scripture: it always has something to say to us and its meaning is inexhaustible. It is like reading a cherished letter or email from a friend or loved one—it reminds you of the significance of that person, the memories you share, and the ways he or she inspires and enriches your life.

The same happens when we read the Bible. The Bible reminds us of what God has done for us and how God wants to be involved in our lives. It reveals the patterns of interaction between God and human beings. The stories and lessons never grow old. We can return to a parable of Jesus, for example, a thousand different times and find new insights each time. If we approach scripture with an open mind and heart, it will never fail to deepen our connection with God.

ACCOMPANYING THE MARGINALIZED

Another way to strengthen our relationship with God is to spend time with the marginalized: those men and women on the margins; those who are sick, suffering, or lonely; or those who are in prison, depressed, or in poverty. The marginalized are those who, for various reasons, find themselves ignored, rejected, or barely noticed by society.

We know Jesus has a special appreciation for those on the margins because Jesus himself tells us this. In the Gospel of Matthew, Jesus says that when we care for the sick, visit those who are imprisoned, feed the hungry, and clothe the naked, we are doing those things for Christ himself. As Jesus says, "Truly I tell you, just as you did it to one of the least of these who are members of my family, you did it to me" (Matt 25:40). When we attend to those whom society rejects, we tend to Jesus. So if we want to be with God, we have to be with those with whom he identifies.

PARTICIPATING IN THE SACRAMENTS

A fourth and vital way Catholics can nourish our relationship with God is to participate in the seven sacraments of the Church: baptism, confirmation, Eucharist, reconciliation (confession), anointing of the sick, holy orders (for example, ordination to the priesthood), and matrimony. The concept of a "sacrament" has rich meaning and, like most subjects in this book, could take up thousands of pages.

Although there are seven official sacraments in the Catholic Church, the basic idea of a sacrament long precedes the formation of those seven. The concept of a sacrament developed in response to this question: "How does the invisible God, who is spirit, become visible and tangible in our world of space and time?"[2] The idea behind a sacramental worldview is that objects, symbols, rituals, and actions—things of this world—can represent and connect us to the invisible God. In short, the sacraments connect heaven with earth, the mundane with the Divine.

The sacraments are essential to the Catholic faith. Catholics believe not only that the sacraments represent and remind us of God's love; but also that they are vehicles for God's love and grace. For example, the sacrament of reconciliation isn't merely symbolic. Rather, Catholics believe that through the ministry of the priest, God channels his love and forgiveness to the one making the confession.

The sacraments are occasions in which Catholics recognize and embrace their spiritual citizenship. Just as going to the gym, practicing yoga, cooking dinner, and other rituals and actions represent other aspects of our lives (other "citizenships," so to speak), the sacraments respond to that part of each of us that needs religious and spiritual nourishment.

Of the seven, there are two that most Catholics can practice on a regular basis: Eucharist (Mass) and reconciliation. In the Eucharist, Catholics recall Jesus' last supper with his apostles and the new life he won for us through his suffering, death, and resurrection. In the celebration of the Eucharist, Catholics receive the body and blood of Jesus—the ultimate participation in the Divine Life.

Through the sacrament of reconciliation, we as sinners can obtain forgiveness for our sins and reconcile with God and the Church. The sacrament "washes us clean" and renews us in Christ.

Relationship at the Heart

These four methods are not the only ways we can nourish our relationships with God. As you explore different ways of being faithful, you'll start to find a path or way of proceeding that works for you. As you search, remember that you are seeking to deepen not an ideology but a relationship. You're seeking to deepen your spiritual citizenship, where heaven, not the world, is the ultimate home. The rules and rituals are designed to support that relationship, not hinder it. We put our faith in a person, not in a rule or an ethical system. And that person or entity is love.

CHAPTER ELEVEN

Being Authentic

So far, we have established that credible reasons support the belief in God's existence, that this God disclosed himself through the writings recorded by the Israelites, that this God entered into relationship with his creation through the person of Jesus Christ, and that this ongoing relationship inspires a change of mind and heart the Gospels refer to as *metanoia*.

While this development might make sense intellectually, it may still be difficult to live out. The language and concepts of the Christian faith, like those of any religion, can be challenging to incorporate into daily life. It might sound heroic or romantic to relinquish all for the sake of Christ, but it also leaves us with questions. What, precisely, is God asking of us? What does it mean to undergo conversion? As we have discussed, the world of the New Testament is very different from the world in which we live today. How, then, do

What do we do ?

we frame our relationships with Jesus in ways that speak to our twenty-first century experiences?

The True and False Selves

Our relationship with God relates to the concept of the true self. Put in its simplest terms, God calls us to our true selves, while evil and worldly influences lure us away from our true selves and toward our false selves. The more we grow closer to God, the more we cultivate our true selves. As Fr. James Martin notes,

> God desires for us to be the persons we were created to be: to be simply and purely ourselves, and in this state to love God and to let ourselves be loved by God. It is a double journey, really: finding God means allowing ourselves to be found by God. And finding our true selves means allowing God to find and reveal our true selves to us.[1]

In other words, in finding ourselves, we find God. The Catholic Bishops at the Second Vatican Council expressed it like this: "When [men and women] are drawn to think about their real selves they turn to those deep recesses of their being where God who probes the heart awaits them, and where they themselves decide their own destiny in the sight of God."[2]

The search for the true self rests upon the truth that the human being is vulnerable and complex. Though we speak of an "I" in the singular, this "I" is actually a plurality. Each of us is made up of many "selves," and those selves compete for attention and face many shaping forces. It starts early. You might remember your school days and the different groups of kids that appeared to be popular. If you didn't feel cool enough, you might have tried to alter your behavior to match what they did. Perhaps you tried to appear more bookish, or more athletic, or more musical than you really were. During my grade school days, I remember pretending to like certain clothes and bands for the sake of being popular.

Regardless of the age, we always feel the pull of different ways of being. In my twenties, I used to ponder making enough money to drive luxury cars and live in a big house, but then I found myself admiring those who lacked that wealth but who had chosen careers they loved. I would recall my Catholic education and my desire to be faithful to God and grow anxious. Who, exactly, was I? What was I supposed to want? What was the self I was supposed to be?

Eventually, it became clear that the "I" was less a single point of light and more like a galaxy of desires, feelings, and emotions. As I stepped outside these selves and placed them under the microscope of prayer, I saw that some of the selves were more artificial than others. They were selves I had created out of fear, out of a desire to please, or out of a desire to be seen as successful. On many days, I labored to be the backslapping lawyer, the young professional who could hobnob with other businessmen, walking into a room where I didn't know anybody and walking out with five clients.

But that role created a feeling of discomfort. At that point in my life, it didn't feel natural, and as long as I labored to live it, I felt divided. Sitting in my office or driving home from work, I would sometimes think, "This is not who God made me to be. I was not put on this earth to do what I'm doing right now." In my frustration, I began to sense what many spiritual writers have spoken of: an inner landscape where multiple selves strain for attention.

After months of reflection, I decided that I was not, at least at that time, called to be an attorney. My true self required a change of direction. Once I began teaching scripture and leading retreats, counseling students through the storms of high school social life and advising them on college applications, I began to feel at peace almost overnight. My roles came naturally and didn't leave me depressed and frustrated, wondering what else life had to offer. I became friendlier, more patient, and more giving of my time. I had no desire to be anywhere other than where I was. I felt joyful and excited, fully alive. It felt like the characters within my "I" were integrated. Although I couldn't quite figure it out at the time, later I would come to realize that I was beginning to experience my true self.

Once we start to conceive of discipleship in terms of finding the true self, we see how this theme opens up the interpretation of scripture. Consider again the story we've been working with throughout this book, the story of the rich young man. Christ urges the man to sell his possessions, give money to the poor, and follow him. While we often read this story in view of its economic impact, maybe feeling sorry for the man for having to give up so much, our interpretation changes in light of discussions about the true self.

If we see Christ as calling the man to his true self, we can see that the man's wealth might be contributing to the ongoing embodiment of a false self. Perhaps the man, were he really to examine the matter, is yearning for a different life but hasn't reflected enough to realize it. Perhaps his concern over money keeps him trapped and isolated. In this view, Christ is not calling the man to something strange, but rather to freedom. He is calling him to a self that isn't restless, a self that doesn't carry persistent spiritual misgivings.

Becoming an Authentic Person

Finding your true self will take time. It will involve the assistance of other people, especially friends and family who care about you and who can offer a patient, loving ear during your frustrating times.

It may also involve a period of trial and error, a time of wandering and testing. Sometimes we have to "try on" different selves to see how they fit. And, to be most accurate, it's not the case that the true self corresponds to a single lifestyle or career. You might be a mother, a doctor, and a pianist. You might be a father, a lawyer, and a husband. The search for the true self, in other words, is not about condensing the roles to which we are called. As of now, I am a husband, teacher, sibling, writer, and son. However, my roles and responsibilities will change throughout my life. My true self is not identical to one role or career, but it's related to, and impacts, all roles and careers. My true self could be compatible with returning to the practice of law, but my true self would not be best served by becoming a pilot. I have gifts and talents better directed to other projects and professions.

Maintaining fidelity to this true self is a lifelong project. As we discussed in chapter 2, the world presents many alluring options for how to be and who to become. There are countless models of success, and the world's distractions and temptations never cease. But that's part of the delight of existence. There is excitement in searching for and discovering the true self. It allows you to meet different people, to sample careers and professions, and to relish the richness of human endeavors. Even when you fail, even if you get stuck in a career you hate or reach a cul-de-sac professionally, you can use that experience for the benefit of others.

A very successful lawyer once told me about a deposition he gave when he was in his late twenties, when he was a young attorney. He said he tried to be aggressive, maybe even ruthless, with the witness. After the deposition, on a long drive back to the airport, he was in tears. He was ashamed of how he acted, and he decided he would never do that again. He didn't want to be that kind of lawyer.

Although he was ashamed of himself then, he now treats that episode as a teachable moment. He shares it with young lawyers to help them understand what it means to be not only an authentic lawyer but also an authentic person. He teaches them, I believe, about the search for the true self. When we find this self, we begin to experience the person that God has created us to be.

CHAPTER TWELVE

Doubt and Despair

Within a few days of his accident, it became clear that Greg's injuries were so traumatic that doctors would not be able to save him. Greg died on Palm Sunday—a week after his fall.

While the news of his death was devastating, for those of us who had been visiting the hospital and who were familiar with his condition, it was not a shock. We knew his body was failing.

Greg was only seventeen and only two months away from his high school graduation. He was a smart, caring, and optimistic young man who made friends easily and welcomed others with a smile. His death seemed so tragic, so unfair, such a violation against all the goodness of the world.

In the aftermath of the funeral, our community fell fully into the inquiries of the 3 a.m. phone call. We prayed for a miracle and none came. How could this be the result of a God who loves and cares for us? Was it God's fault? The New Testament speaks of a God who, in Jesus Christ, heals the sick, even raising some of his contemporaries from the dead. Why didn't God save Greg? Those questions stem from the most challenging issues we face on the journey of faith. And they strike like an earthquake.

At times, everything seems settled. We have constructed our faith brick by brick, experience by experience, and book by book. We have pondered, prayed, and accepted the reasons for God's existence we noted in chapter 5. Maybe our faith in Jesus has been developing as well. We might even have begun to pray to him, starting to establish the divine–human friendship that at one point seemed so elusive.

And then we experience a death, an illness, a betrayal, or a great injustice, and we fall into frustration, grief, confusion, or sorrow. All the work we had done to build up our faith appears to have been a waste. Arguments for God's existence or previous intuitions of divine love seem to be no more than wishful thinking. One of the most powerful descriptions I've read of such an experience comes from the Catholic historian Eamon Duffy, who wrote about the death of his good friend. Describing that experience years later, he wrote,

> It turned out to be the most traumatic event of my life. Never before or since has anything so terrible happened to me. I still do not know why I was so affected, but in the weeks after his death I woke up night after night, drenched in icy sweat, swept by wave after wave of nauseating physical fear of death; my own, my wife's, our new-born son's. Not fear that somehow we might die soon, unexpectedly; just a horrifying realization that one day there would be nothing; that our hopes, our preoccupations, our beliefs would be simply brushed aside, shown up for the meaningless treadmill they had always been. And with the horror came the realization that God was gone; there was no God, and I had no faith. All the conditioning, all the arguments

and emotional scaffolding I had built around and into my life were as if they had never been.[1]

Duffy's faith in God eventually returned, and in the process, he gained greater insight into the nature of Jesus and the Church, which we will examine below. But it took some time, and for a long while, he was shaken.

Joseph Ratzinger (the future Pope Benedict XVI) talked about such dark moments in his outstanding book *Introduction to Christianity*. There are times, he said, when life becomes so difficult that "wherever one looks, only the bottomless abyss of nothingness can be seen."[2]

I have no experience of the death of a child, but the abyss of nothingness is precisely what seems to confront those who do. Though I have not asked Greg's parents, I imagine they felt what theologian Nicholas Wolterstorff did after his twenty-five-year-old son died in a hiking accident. Wolterstorff wrote, "There's a hole in the world now. In the place where he was, there's now just nothing. A center, like no other, of memory and hope and knowledge and affection which once inhabited this earth is gone. Only a gap remains."[3]

We must acknowledge honestly the pain that life can present. It would be careless not to. Though not every person will undergo the death of a child, all of us undergo periods where everything seems to fall apart, where the optimistic affirmations of faith and the general support structure it normally provides dissolve. At times, the call to follow Jesus, the search for the true self, and the peace that Jesus promises seem to be part of a project that is going nowhere.

In the aftermath of these periods, what are we to do? How do we work through these trials in our spiritual lives? Do they signal the end for our faith journeys, or is there a way to make a breakthrough? How can we helpfully think about those times when it seems impossible to trust in God; indeed, when it seems God may not exist?

It's Okay to Doubt

Doubt is okay. The Catholic faith acknowledges the challenge of unbelief, seeing it not as a problem or a deficiency but as an element inherent in the human journey. Scripture echoes this when the psalmist writes, "How long, O LORD? Will you forget me forever? How long will you hide your face from me? How long must I bear pain in my soul, and have sorrow in my heart all day long? How long shall my enemy be exalted over me?" (Ps 13:1–2). Pope Benedict XVI also reminds us that "faith is always a path. As long as we live we are on the way, and on that account faith is always under pressure and under threat."[4] Faith in God is always vulnerable. As we noted in chapter 2, there are always going to be forces that challenge religious faith and attempt to weaken it, that attempt to make us forget or ignore what we had previously believed.[5]

Although this vulnerability can occasionally leave us reeling, it can also be liberating. To go through life without doubting in God would impose a daunting psychological burden. Unfortunately, many people think that doubting God is a flaw, a weakness, or even sinful. On the contrary, doubt is part of the faith journey in the same way that storms and choppy waters are part of the voyage across an ocean. It's part of faith in the way that sickness and illness are part of the human body. We don't say that someone should abandon the pursuit of health simply because they contract the flu. We don't say that health doesn't exist because someone gets sick. In the same way, we don't need to abandon our pursuit of faith because we struggle to believe or because God feels absent.

120

Openness and Empathy

A crisis of faith can open our lives to the insights and the lives of others. For Christians, the journey of faith is not made in isolation; it is a communal undertaking. We are inherently social beings, and we draw strength and sustenance from the richness of our relationships.

When we find ourselves frozen in despair, we are invited to look beyond ourselves and transcend our own often limited, and limiting, cycles of thoughts. Maybe we can call a friend or family member with whom we haven't spoken for some time, so that our own sadness becomes the vehicle for connecting with others. Maybe we can read a book that offers wisdom for our wounds or consult the perspectives of another religious tradition, not as a means of replacing our Christian faith, but as a way of supporting it. Sometimes writings from other religious traditions can provide a fresh look at our own. For example, the practice of mindfulness, which has a special place in Buddhist traditions, can be helpful during anxious times. It can calm the thoughts so that Jesus can enter.

Similarly, spiritual sorrow can cultivate empathy. When things are going well, we tend to think that the world is wonderful. While it's good to be positive, our cheerful attitudes can obscure the heartaches that afflict others. But in the moments of despair when we ask, "How can this be? Why me?" we identify with the troubles that countless people throughout the world endure every day. Our doubts tune us into a new frequency of human connection.

Purification

When our prayers appear to go unanswered or when life takes a jarring turn, we know definitively that we cannot confine

God to human categories or treat him as a divine valet; that is, as a being that should respond to our demands. As the *Catechism of the Catholic Church* instructs,

> God transcends all creatures. We must therefore continually purify our language of everything in it that is limited, image-bound or imperfect, if we are not to confuse our image of God—"the inexpressible, the incomprehensible, the invisible, the ungraspable"— with our human representations. Our human words always fall short of the mystery of God.[6]

Doubt and uncertainty can be the means of purification. Perhaps we have treated God like a spiritual ATM machine. Perhaps we have thought we have access to God that others lack, or that our prayers have priority over the prayers of others. Our questioning and our pain, however, remind us of words from the Hebrew Scriptures: "For my thoughts are not your thoughts, nor are your ways my ways, says the LORD. For as the heavens are higher than the earth, so are my ways higher than your ways and my thoughts than your thoughts" (Isa 55:8–9). God remains incomprehensible. God does not bend to our timelines or plans.

Would you want it any other way? Would you want the Almighty Creator, the source of the magnificent universe, to conform to human expectations, to our personal whims? Is that the kind of God worth praying to, worth giving our lives to? No! It wouldn't be God at all.

Doubt and the True Self

Doubt draws us beyond and deepens knowledge of the self. Difficulties with God leave us with the questions of the 3 a.m. phone call: Who am I? What do I want? What is truth? Our questioning can lead us to a more precise awareness of our strengths, weaknesses, motivations, and knowledge. During my late twenties, while straining to discern my life and career, I recall pleading with God to "make me happy," to let me settle into my legal career without discomfort. When that didn't happen, depression and frustration formed, and I would accuse God of not listening to me. Week after week, I would attend Mass frustrated that my external blessings were not translating to inner contentment.

God's silence gave me the chance to examine my background theories and presumptions about God and the good life. Was I asking for the right things? Did I want to practice law? Was God calling me to be a lawyer? Was I living as a disciple of Jesus? Over time, I saw that I had started to treat God as half personal assistant, half therapist. He was supposed to meet my demands. He was supposed to make me feel good and prevent me from feeling any uneasiness.

This was ridiculous, for that kind of God is not God. It was a reality created from my own insecurities and compulsions: I wanted a scapegoat, and in looking for one, I was making God in my image. Scripture, however, tells us that God makes us in *his* image.

I realized that a major change was needed. As I sat with my frustration, I realized that I had been praying for God to accommodate a desire that, in the end, I didn't want. God redirected my restlessness toward another opportunity, but I began to sense this only because I had to wait. I had to be patient. God could have ended my questioning overnight, but in letting me wonder, doubt, question, and fume, he taught me that breakthroughs in the spiritual life take time.

Unity with Jesus

Jesus, too, had his doubts and spiritual difficulties. Pope Benedict once observed, "Jesus struggles with the Father. He struggles with himself. And he struggles for us. He experiences anguish before the power of death."[7]

Jesus may not have doubted God's existence, but the human side of Jesus felt God's absence. As he hung on the cross, he exclaimed, "My God, my God, why have you forsaken me?" (Matt 27:46). In other words: *Where have you gone? Why have you abandoned me?*

If Jesus felt this way, we know that we need not flee doubt. Even when we feel near our breaking points, we know that we are not alone.

Our doubt is an opportunity to deepen our faith, to teach us what it means to take our religious beliefs seriously. Although the death of his friend shattered Eamon Duffy's faith for a time, he continued to go to Mass. Eventually, he made a breakthrough that he later wrote about in his book *Faith of our Fathers*:

All this time I had carried on going to Mass, though I didn't know what I was doing there. And it was there, in its celebration of the death of Jesus (and what an extraordinary idea the *celebration* of a death seemed), that I found something by which I could establish some sort of bearing on my turmoil. For as I knelt there rather numbly, week by week, it dawned on me that the Mass began from the point at which I had now arrived. Here, in a ritual grown commonplace to me by long acquaintance, there was an unblinking contemplation that men and women died, often horribly, that good is defeated, that power crushes tenderness, that lies swallow up the truth. And in the face of that acknowledgment, in the face of the cross, the Mass proclaimed a celebration, an affirmation of the unquenchable life of love. Out of death—and not just the death of Jesus, but out of *my* death...it asserted our right to rejoice. It did so because there had once been a man whose trust in the loving reality that underlay the world was so total that in the face of his own destruction he could still call that reality Father; whose death was not an end to his loving, but the means of its infinite expansion.[8]

The Mass, the ritual where we Catholics remember the life, death, and resurrection of Jesus, acknowledged and reframed Duffy's tribulation. It didn't evade it. It didn't ignore it. The Mass announced that despair did not have the last word. The faith of Christ had shown that death was not final. Jesus' total entrustment to the Father, despite his anguish on the cross, became Duffy's light during his dark time.

Duffy's experience demonstrates the ways that our doubt can strengthen our faith and deepen our connection with God. Before the death of his friend, Duffy thought he had faith figured out. As Duffy began his career as a history professor, he said he "was not only religious," but "was *successfully* religious."[9] Duffy had grown up in the Catholic faith and had studied Church history in graduate school. But his faith had never been tested like it was when his friend died. It went from being academic to being something real and concrete. It forced him to wrestle with the meaning of Jesus and the Mass, to really and truly appreciate what it meant to believe that God had become a human being.

Doubt and God's Love

Our capacity to doubt results from God's love. To have certainty, to know everything about the mysteries that leave us sometimes fearful and on edge, would impose a burden and responsibility that would crush our psyches.

Doubt usually arises because we don't have precise answers to the questions of the 3 a.m. phone call: Does God exist? How did the universe come about? And, how can a loving God allow evil? But once we ask those questions, it becomes arbitrary to limit responses to only the information that would satisfy our specific inquiries. We cannot act as if we are students who, when reviewing gaps in our notes, want to know only what will be on the exam. If we are going to seek answers to the most fundamental questions, we have to be willing, both logically and morally, to accept the implications of those answers and the hard truths they convey.

This means that we can't desire to know merely the good things, the things that confirm the optimistic narratives about our lives we intuitively craft. I can't seek to reconcile evil with a loving God and expect a response fit for Facebook and Twitter. Instead, I have to be willing to know what evil truly is. I have to be willing to know what Christ knows, to inhabit, in some sense, the mind of God.

But are humans prepared for this? Would you want this burden? Are you willing to know what Christ knows? And would it even contribute to your peace of mind? This would be analogous to receiving the daily intelligence briefings that the President of the United States reads, the news about threats and potential attacks from around the globe. It is "inside" knowledge, but it is haunting knowledge. The President reads things that would terrify most Americans, maybe even halt normal activity. But we don't have to bear that burden. American citizens remain ignorant of much of what goes on in the world, but that frees us to go about our lives and attend to our communities.

It's the same with respect to God's knowledge. Were we to know what God knows, we'd be overwhelmed by the responsibility it would place on us. In our doubt, we are free to go about our lives without feeling the weight of both the divine and earthly kingdoms. For this we should be grateful.

While this may be a fruitful way of treating doubt in the spiritual life, it doesn't always bring relief. Sometimes there is simply nothing that seems to help: we feel stuck, alone, abandoned. We can give God only our sorrow and our grief.

This is what it means to be human. This is part of the faith journey. However, although doubts and struggles will be with us always, they do not have to signal the end of the faith journey, the end of our relationship with God. As he worked through his own view of God after his son's death, Nicolas Wolterstorrf wrote,

> When I survey this gigantic intricate world, I cannot believe that it just came about. I do not mean that I have some good arguments for its being made and that I believe in the arguments. I mean that this conviction wells up irresistibly within me when I contemplate the world. The experiment of trying to abolish it does not work. When looking at the heavens, I cannot manage to believe that they do not declare the glory of God. When looking at the earth, I cannot bring off the attempt to believe that it does not display his handiwork.
>
> And when I read the New Testament and look into the material surrounding it, I am convinced that the man Jesus of Nazareth was raised from the dead. In that, I see the sign that he was more than a prophet. He was the Son of God.
>
> Faith is a footbridge that you don't know will hold you up over the chasm until you're forced to walk out onto it.[10]

At times, this footbridge appears terrifyingly fragile. Sometimes we might be able to muster only a dim hope that things will get better, but if, within our pain, we find a way to listen, we also might hear the voice of the One, without whom we'd have no voice to make our cry. We might gain an insight or a new perspective that, as it did for Eamon Duffy, renews our bond with God—like a muscle, a bond that has become stronger by being first torn down.

Conclusion

Writing a book is like taking a series of photographs. A writer captures vignettes of an endless landscape that, depending upon the angle, can vary from one day to another. Writing requires tough decisions about when to zoom in and when to pull back, and about what to keep, add, and edit.

Consequently, this book comprises only a limited portrait of a complex, fascinating, beautiful, and mysterious terrain. There is much that can be said about the nature of the Church, the doctrine of the Trinity, the seven sacraments, the role of sin in our lives, Catholic social teaching, the lives of the saints, and other topics that are essential to the Catholic Church and the journey of faith that deserve more thorough investigation. A mature spirituality must engage these topics in order to cultivate a richer view of what it means to enter into relationship with Jesus and the Christian community. These issues provide the themes and support structures for a sophisticated, informed, and intentional spiritual citizenship, where heaven remains the ultimate horizon.

A mature faith must also consider the status and contributions of other religions. The first

Christians, including Jesus, were Jews, and Christians, like the Jews, believe the Hebrew Scriptures to be inspired by God. While Christians will always proclaim the truth and message of Jesus, the Church acknowledges that other religions offer valuable truths about God and the human condition. Without abandoning faith in Christ or participation in the Catholic Church, Catholics should situate their understanding of Catholicism within the broader panorama of spiritual searching.

Why Faith?

Faith is intrinsic to our lives. We cannot live without it. We are constantly entrusting ourselves to people, expectations, conditions, and hoped-for futures. For us to live, we must believe. Accordingly, the question is not whether we will have faith, but what the scope and content of that faith will be. We know we have to put our faith in friends and in family members, in doctors and in medicine, in health inspectors and in pilots, in the beating of our own hearts and in the path of the sun. We even, as Paul Davies argues, have to put our faith in the laws of science.

In other words, we must put our faith in the things of this world. But then we can ask these questions: To what else, or to whom else, will this faith extend? Are there grounds, are there credible reasons, for letting our faith reach a dimension that people categorize as "religious," a dimension that involves the being we call God?

Christians believe that the foundational entrustment that is required of every life must extend beyond this world. Christians believe this not because of wishful thinking, not for political or psychological reasons, but because the nature of the universe, historical developments, and the witness of lives across the centuries strongly suggest that God not only exists but has made himself known, first through the writings of the Israelites and then most definitively through Jesus Christ.

Certainly, this evidence does not remove all doubt; it is not the kind of evidence that gives us certainty. We don't believe in God once we have, or because we have, foolproof data that he exists. There has to be an initial willingness to believe, an initial openness to the reality of God. Moreover, faith in God and in Jesus Christ remains a gift from God himself. We cannot force a relationship with Jesus. He comes to us on his terms. If we find ourselves sensing a spiritual presence, or if we find ourselves motivated to pray, it is because God himself has drawn us to him.

If we remain open to this gift, if we let ourselves be ushered into the mystery of Jesus Christ, this faith relationship will transform our lives and offer a spiritual rebirth. It will give us a share in the kingdom of God. As we undergo *metanoia*—the conversion of mind and heart to which Christ calls us—we become free from habits and behaviors that have held us captive. We begin to see that our lives are best lived as one long expression of thanks to the Creator whose love enables us to be.

Though at times daunting, even frightening, faith in Christ opens us to the hidden contours of the "true self," the person that God made each of us to be. Once we take Christ as our guide, we have a foundation from which to evaluate the lifestyles, careers, and personalities that lure us without ceasing. Faith in Christ is the gravity that keeps us in spiritual orbit.

Faith is the recognition that we remain always within the horizon of uncertainty, which frees us from the compulsion to try to get everything—all the decisions and choices and circumstances of life—perfect and certain. We are not equipped with all-knowing minds, and we cannot be expected to live as if we are. We pursue truth as far as we can, trusting that God's life and love—his grace—will make up for our mistakes and inabilities. Faith in God, therefore, relieves us from the burden of being the

Lord of our own lives. In the words of a common expression, we can "let go and let God."

Faith in Christ keeps our minds on the goal for which we have been created. Anchored by belief in the resurrection, Christians know that earth is only a temporary home. We are born to glorify God and live with him forever. This truth, as we know, does not anesthetize all wounds. But it is the backdrop against which we live and love, and it is the reason that everyone grieving Greg's death can nonetheless say, Though he is not here, he is not gone; though his earthly life has ended, another has begun.

Notes

INTRODUCTION

1. Second Vatican Council, *Nostra Aetate*, no. 2.

CHAPTER 1

1. Pope John Paul II, *Fides et Ratio*, September 14, 1998, no. 1.
2. Ibid., nos. 1, 4.

CHAPTER 2

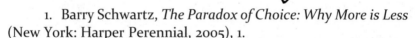

1. Barry Schwartz, *The Paradox of Choice: Why More is Less* (New York: Harper Perennial, 2005), 1.
2. Stanley Kunitz, "The Layers," in *The Collected Poems* (New York: W. W. Norton & Company, 2002).
3. This isn't to say the same holds for their parents.
4. Gary Marcus and Christof Koch, "The Future of Brain Implants," *Wall Street Journal*, March 14, 2014, http://online.wsj.com/news/articles/SB100014240527023049149045794355929 81780528.

CHAPTER 3

1. When we consider this basic act of entrustment that all of us make, the understanding of faith in the Letter to the Hebrews makes more sense: "Now faith is the assurance of things hoped for, the conviction of things not seen" (Heb 11:1).
2. Pope John Paul II, *Fides et Ratio*, no. 31.

3. Paul Davies, "Taking Science on Faith," *New York Times*, November 24, 2007, http://www.nytimes.com/2007/11/24/opinion/24davies.html?pagewanted=all&_r=0.

4. Ibid.

5. Paul Davies, *The Mind of God: The Scientific Basis for a Rational World* (New York: Simon and Schuster/Orion Productions, 1992), 81.

CHAPTER 5

1. If the created world did not possess intelligibility, it would be unintelligible: incapable of being deciphered and mastered.

2. This doesn't mean that we have figured out nature completely. Unknowns remain, but they remain discoverable only because of the world's intelligibility.

3. Cf. C. S. Lewis, *The Case for Christianity* (New York: Scribner Paper Fiction, 1989), 32.

4. It's important to add that many scientists who don't believe in God would say this apparent design in nature came about through Darwinian natural selection with no involvement of a Divine Reality. But we can still ask the following: What empowered or enabled natural selection itself? What is the source of nature's ability to rid itself of what doesn't work and keep what does work? These questions lead inevitably back to where we began: toward the existence of an intelligent mind.

5. Robert Spitzer, *New Proofs for the Existence of God: Contributions of Contemporary Physics and Philosophy* (Grand Rapids, MI: Wm. B. Eerdmans Publishing Co., 2010), 52.

6. Ibid., 5–6.

7. Ian G. Barbour, *Religion and Science* (San Francisco: HarperOne, 1997), 204.

8. "What is the 'fine-tuning' of the universe, and how does it serve as a 'pointer to God'?" *Biologos*, accessed October 10, 2014, http://biologos.org/questions/fine-tuning.

9. Ibid.

10. Barbour, *Religion and Science*, 205.

11. Ibid.

12. Ibid.

13. Ibid.

14. C. S. Lewis put it this way: "The moment you say that one set of moral ideas can be better than another, you are, in fact, measuring them both by a standard, saying that one of them conforms to that standard more nearly than the other. But the standard that measures two things is something different from either. You are, in fact, comparing them both with some Real Morality, admitting that there is such a thing as a real Right, independent of what people think, and that some people's ideas get nearer to that real Right than others." *Mere Christianity* (San Francisco: HarperSanFrancisco, 2015), 14.

15. Francis S. Collins, *The Language of God: A Scientist Presents Evidence for Belief* (New York: Free Press, 2006).

16. Francis Collins, interview by PBS, accessed August 3, 2014, http://www.pbs.org/wgbh/questionofgod/voices/collins.html.

17. Ibid.

18. Ibid.

19. Ibid.

20. Ibid.

21. Ibid.

CHAPTER 6

1. See Fr. Robert Barron, "Fr. Robert Barron on Faith and Reason," from Word on Fire, https://www.youtube.com/watch?v=GcH_5Iecu5s; and "Fr. Robert Barron on What Faith Is and What Faith Isn't," from Word on Fire, https://www.youtube.com/watch?v=m_4PSgFjtvI.

2. Although the Bible is commonly thought of as one book, the word *Bible* derives from a Greek word that means "books." Many books make up the Bible, not only one.

3. Leon R. Kass, *The Beginning of Wisdom: Reading Genesis* (Chicago: University of Chicago Press, 2006), xi.

4. Ibid., xi–xii.

5. Ibid., xii.

6. Pope Benedict XVI, *Verbum Domini*, no. 6.

7. Carey Walsh, *Chasing Mystery: A Catholic Biblical Theology* (Collegeville, MN: Michael Glazier, 2012), 51.

8. The word *testament* comes from a Greek word meaning "covenant." A covenant refers to an agreement between two people or two parties; it's a word that also connotes a promise between two parties.

9. Richard P. McBrien, *Catholicism* (San Francisco: HarperOne, 1994), 350. (Emphasis in original.)

CHAPTER 7

1. "Therefore say to the house of Israel, Thus says the Lord GOD: Will you defile yourselves after the manner of your ancestors and go astray after their detestable things? When you offer your gifts and make your children pass through the fire, you defile yourselves with all your idols to this day" (Ezek 20:30–31).

2. Thomas P. Rausch and Catherine E. Clifford, *Catholicism in the Third Millennium* (Collegeville, MN: Michael Glazier, 2003), 30–31.

3. Although we may casually say "Jesus Christ," it is more accurate to say "Jesus the Christ," which means, "Jesus the Anointed One" or "Jesus the Messiah."

4. In the Old Testament, the title "Messiah" was applied to kings, prophets, and priests, figures who were anointed prior to their missions. Eventually, the Israelites began to expect a historical figure that would essentially combine all three roles.

5. Antony Flew, *There Is a God: How the World's Most Notorious Atheist Changed His Mind* (San Francisco: HarperOne, 2007), Appendix B, 187.

6. Luke Timothy Johnson, *The Real Jesus: The Misguided Quest for the Historical Jesus and the Truth of the Traditional Gospels* (San Francisco: HarperSanFrancisco, 1996), 123.

7. Bart D. Ehrman, "Did Jesus Exist?" *Huffington Post*, March 20, 2012, http://www.huffingtonpost.com/bart-d-ehrman/did-jesus-exist_b_1349544.html.

8. Johnson, *The Real Jesus*, 134.

9. Ibid.

10. N. T. Wright, "The Self-Revelation of God in Human History: A Dialogue on Jesus with N. T. Wright," in Flew, *There is a God*, Appendix B, 199.

11. Ibid., 200.

12. Ibid.

13. Ibid., 201.

14. Ibid., 202.

15. Ibid.

16. Ibid., 203–4.

17. Ibid., 209.

18. Johnson, *The Real Jesus*, 136.

19. Even if there were people who were standing inside the tomb of Jesus, staring at his dead body, who then observed him rise from death, we'd still run into the same problems of credibility that we noted in chapter 4. How could those people possibly convince others of what they saw? What evidence could they provide to prove to the world that they had actually witnessed the resurrection? The devoted skeptic could always accuse them of lying, of being delusional, or of being insane. At some point, that skeptic would have to be willing to believe in the possibility of the resurrection for the evidence of such an event to have any chance at changing minds.

CHAPTER 8

1. Joseph Cardinal Ratzinger, *Introduction to Christianity* (San Francisco: Ignatius Press, 2004, original English translation 1969), 205.

2. Pope Francis, *The Church of Mercy* (Chicago: Loyola Press, 2014), 71.

3. Robert Barron, *And Now I See: A Theology of Transformation* (New York: Crossroad Publishing, 1998), 8.

4. James Martin, *In Good Company* (Lanham, MD: Sheed & Ward, 2010), 60.

5. Carey Walsh, *Chasing Mystery* (Collegeville, MN: Michael Glazier, 2012), 59.

6. Vocation comes from the Latin word *vocare*, meaning "to call." The Catholic Church teaches that everyone has a unique calling.

CHAPTER 9

1. Barron, *And Now I See*, 5.
2. Saint Ignatius of Loyola, *Personal Writings*, trans. Joseph A. Munitiz and Philip Endean (New York: Penguin Books, 1996), 13.
3. Ibid., 16.

CHAPTER 10

1. Pope Benedict XVI, *Deus Caritas Est*, no. 1.
2. Thomas P. Rausch and Catherine E. Clifford, *Catholicism in the Third Millennium* (Collegeville, MN: Michael Glazier, 2003), 86.

CHAPTER 11

1. James Martin, *Becoming Who You Are: Insights on the True Self from Thomas Merton and Other Saints* (Mahwah, NJ: HiddenSpring, 2006), 22.
2. *Gaudium et Spes*, no. 14.

CHAPTER 12

1. Eamon Duffy, *Faith of Our Fathers* (New York: Bloomsbury Academic, 2006), 5.
2. Joseph Cardinal Ratzinger, *Introduction to Christianity* (San Francisco: Ignatius Press, 2004), 43.
3. Nicholas Wolterstorff, *Lament for a Son* (Grand Rapids, MI: Eerdmans, 1987), 33.
4. Pope Benedict XVI, *God and the World: A Conversation with Peter Seewald* (San Francisco: Ignatius Press, 2003), 36.
5. Our capacity for memory is crucial. We must continue to mark and memorialize and intentionally remember those moments when we have felt God's presence, love, and action. If

we don't, we will be at the mercy of our feelings or bad times and may forget what God had once done for us. This is one reason why the Passover meal is so important for Jews: it is a meal of remembrance; it is a meal that reminds them of God's liberating power. This is also why (in part) the Eucharist is important for Catholics. It's a collective effort to remember the good news and saving mission of Jesus Christ.

6. *Catechism of the Catholic Church*, no. 42.

7. Pope Benedict XVI, "Mass of the Lord's Supper: Homily of His Holiness Benedict XVI" (homily, Basilica of St. John Lateran, April 5, 2012), http://w2.vatican.va/content/benedict-xvi/en/homilies/2012/documents/hf_ben-xvi_hom_20120405_coena-domini.html.

8. Duffy, *Faith of our Fathers*, 7–8.

9. Ibid., 4.

10. Wolterstorff, *Lament for a Son*, 76.

Select Bibliography

CHURCH DOCUMENTS

Catechism of the Catholic Church. 2nd ed. Washington, DC: United States Catholic Conference, 1994.

Second Vatican Council, *Gaudium et Spes*, The Pastoral Constitution on the Church in the Modern World, 1965.

Second Vatican Council, *Nostra Aetate*, The Declaration on the Relation of the Church with Non-Christian Religions, 1965.

Pope Benedict XVI, *Deus Caritas Est*, God Is Love, Washington, DC: United States Catholic Conference, 2006.

Pope Benedict XVI, *Verbum Domini*, The Word of the Lord, Washington, DC: United States Catholic Conference, 2012.

Pope John Paul II, *Fides et Ratio*, Faith and Reason, Washington, DC: United States Catholic Conference, 1998.

GENERAL

Barbour, Ian G. *Religion and Science: Historical and Contemporary Issues*, Gifford Lectures Series. San Francisco: HarperOne, 1997.

Barron, Robert. *And Now I See: A Theology of Transformation.* New York: Crossroad Publishing, 1998.

Collins, Francis S. *The Language of God: A Scientist Presents Evidence for Belief.* New York: Free Press, 2006.

Davies, Paul. *The Mind of God: The Scientific Basis for a Rational World*. New York: Simon and Schuster/Orion Productions, 1992.

———. "Taking Science on Faith." *New York Times*, November 24, 2007.

Duffy, Eamon. *Faith of Our Fathers*. New York: Bloomsbury Academic, 2006.

Flew, Antony. *There Is a God: How the World's Most Notorious Atheist Changed His Mind*. San Francisco: HarperOne, 2007.

Johnson, Luke Timothy. *The Real Jesus: The Misguided Quest for the Historical Jesus and the Truth of the Traditional Gospels*. San Francisco: HarperSanFrancisco, 1996.

Kass, Leon R. *The Beginning of Wisdom: Reading Genesis*. Chicago: University of Chicago Press, 2006.

Lewis, C. S. *Mere Christianity*. San Francisco: HarperSan-Francisco, 2015.

Martin, James. *Becoming Who You Are: Insights on the True Self from Thomas Merton and Other Saints*. Mahwah, NJ: HiddenSpring, 2006.

———. *In Good Company*. Lanham, MD: Sheed & Ward, 2010.

McBrien, Richard P. *Catholicism*. San Francisco: HarperOne, 1994.

Pope Francis. *The Church of Mercy*. Chicago: Loyola Press, 2014.

Ratzinger, Joseph Cardinal. *Introduction to Christianity*. San Francisco: Ignatius Press, 2004. Original English translation 1969.

Rausch, Thomas P., and Catherine E. Clifford. *Catholicism in the Third Millennium*, 2nd ed. Collegeville, MN: Liturgical Press, 2003.

Saint Ignatius of Loyola. *Personal Writings*. Translated by Joseph A. Munitiz and Philip Endean. New York: Penguin Books, 1996.

Schwartz, Barry. *The Paradox of Choice: Why More Is Less*. New York: Harper Perennial, 2005.

Spitzer, Robert. *New Proofs for the Existence of God: Contributions of Contemporary Physics and Philosophy*. Grand Rapids, MI: Wm. B. Eerdmans Publishing Co., 2010.

Walsh, Carey. *Chasing Mystery: A Catholic Biblical Theology*. Collegeville, MN: Michael Glazier, 2012.

Wolterstorff, Nicholas. *Lament for a Son*. Grand Rapids, MI: Eerdmans, 1987.